STUDIES IN ENGLISH LITERATURE No. 6

General Editor

David Daiches

Already published in the series (*continued*):

MARLOWE:
DR. FAUSTUS

by

J. P. BROCKBANK

Professor of English
University of York

EDWARD ARNOLD

© J. P. BROCKBANK 1962

First published 1962 by
Edward Arnold (Publishers) Ltd
41 Bedford Square, London WC1B 3DQ

Reprinted 1965, 1968, 1971, 1974, 1977, 1979

ISBN: 0 7131 5063 7

To my Parents

Printed and bound in Great Britain at
The Camelot Press Ltd, Southampton

General Preface

The object of this series is to provide studies of individual novels, plays and groups of poems and essays which are known to be widely read by students. The emphasis is on clarification and evaluation; biographical and historical facts, while they may be discussed when they throw light on particular elements in a writer's work, are generally subordinated to critical discussion. What kind of work is this? What exactly goes on here? How good is this work, and why? These are the questions that each writer will try to answer.

It should be emphasized that these studies are written on the assumption that the reader has already read carefully the work discussed. The objective is not to enable students to deliver opinions about works they have not read, nor is it to provide ready-made ideas to be applied to works that have been read. In one sense all critical interpretation can be regarded as foisting opinions on readers, but to accept this is to deny the advantages of any sort of critical discussion directed at students or indeed at anybody else. The aim of these studies is to provide what Coleridge called in another context 'aids to reflection' about the works discussed. The interpretations are offered as suggestive rather than as definitive, in the hope of stimulating the reader into developing further his own insights. This is after all the function of all critical discourse among sensible people.

Because of the interest which this kind of study has aroused, it has been decided to extend it first from merely English literature to include also some selected works of American literature and now further to include selected works in English by Commonwealth writers. The criterion will remain that the book studied is important in itself and is widely read by students.

DAVID DAICHES

Acknowledgments

The commentary on the play is indebted at many points to the editions of F. S. Boas (1932) and W. W. Greg (*Marlowe's* Dr. Faustus, *Parallel Texts*, 1950). Quotations and references follow W. W. Greg's 'Conjectural Reconstruction' of 1950. Quotations from plays by Marlowe other than *Dr. Faustus* are from C. F. Tucker Brooke (ed.), *The Works of Christopher Marlowe* (1910).

Contents

1. Perspectives of Criticism

Like an alexandrite stone, *Dr. Faustus* changes its colour and depth with the source and quality of the light cast upon it. It assimilates many energies, ideas and conventions from its own time and from a more distant past, and if these are explored in the right way and seen in proper perspective, they qualify and sharpen our varying responses and compel us to explain them more precisely.

From Simon Magus to Faustus

When Marlowe took up the English Faust-book *The Historie of the Damnable Life and Deserved Death of Dr. John Faustus* by 'P.F.', he saw that it already had a satisfying rightness of design, and while he transformed the tract into a tragedy, he kept the outline. What pretends to be a history is indeed a myth—a story shaped by the imagination in the course of time to embody an important truth about the human condition. The Faust-myth is a warning against pride and presumption, but at the same time it hints at the frustration of high aspiration by a hostile moral order.[1]

The earliest stories concern Simon Magus, usually taken to be the same Simon as he who tried to buy from the Apostles the power to confer the gift of the Holy Ghost (*Acts* viii). They tell of his rhetorical skill and knowledge of astronomy, his conjuring before the Emperor at Rome, his apotheosis of a re-incarnated Helen of Troy and finally of his being dashed down when Peter frustrated his attempted flight to heaven. Simon, like Faustus, tried his brains to gain a deity.

Most of the Simonian material found in the play comes by way of the Faust-book (including the turning of a horse into hay and the riding in a

---

[1] See also Beatrice Daw Brown, 'Marlowe, Faustus, and Simon Magus', *PMLA* 54, 1939, to which this section is indebted. For source material see P. M. Palmer and R. P. More, *The Sources of the Faust Tradition from Simon Magus to Lessing* (1936). *Acts of Peter* is reprinted in *The Apocryphal Books of the New Testament* (O.U.P.). Accounts of the historical Faustus are given in J. Bakeless, *The Tragical History of Marlowe* (2 vols. 1942), and E. M. Butler, *The Myth of the Magus* (1948).

fiery chariot), but two incidents (the demon dogs and the trick beheading) with a few faint verbal parallels have been taken as evidence that Marlowe had read two of the earlier Simonian documents—the apocryphal *Acts of Peter* and the *Recognitions* of Clement of Rome. The importance of these works for us, and possibly for Marlowe, is that they raise in acute and spectacular form a number of questions about the nature of good and evil power that meet us again in the play. The *Acts of Peter* shows Simon ('the angel of Satan') overreached in miracles, and the *Recognitions* shows him outwitted in debate. But both give the devil his due. Simon is learned, intelligent and highly accomplished, and only a saint can prevent him from taking in 'simple men'. Simon makes converts by 'art magic' (he flies over the gates of Rome) and Peter wins them back by 'signs and wonders' (he makes a dead fish swim). In a decisive and perhaps allegoric episode Peter brings fully to life a corpse that could only nod at Simon's bidding, and it seems that magic is only a travesty of true miracle.

But although Peter finally vindicates his power from Christ, Simon's from the devil wins many local victories. At one point, 'smitten with sharp afflictions' Peter is compelled to recognise 'the divers arts and temptations of the devil'. He remembers that Satan compelled Judas to deliver up Christ, hardened the heart of Herod, inflamed Pharaoh against Moses and emboldened Caiaphas to give Christ to the unrighteous multitude. 'Even until now,' he says to Satan, 'thou shootest at innocent souls with thy poisonous arrows.' Marlowe's play may be read in the spirit of this reluctant but awed tribute to the devil's power, taking as starting-point Mephostophilis's last speech to Faustus, where he claims to have turned the leaves of the Bible and 'damned up' the passage to heaven. Just as the play has no saint to outplay the devil at his own game of sorcery, so (it may seem) does it leave the soul without defences against the devil's 'poisonous arrows'.

Simon's own followers called him 'the great Power of God' (*Acts* viii. 10) and the *Recognitions* says he wished to be thought Christ 'and to be called the Standing One'. The God he stood for, however, was not the Biblical God, but a remote ineffable being 'incomprehensible and unknown to all'. The world, he said, was not created by God but by envious angels and powers who did what they could to frustrate His will. Salvation is a liberation from the laws that the jealous Old Testament Creator has imposed, and a reaching upward to the 'bodiless and infinite light' of the True God, the source of all wisdom and power. The Creator showed weakness in forbidding Adam to touch the Tree of Knowledge, and perversity in condemning man to death for his disobedience; for it is man's virtue that, knowing good and evil, he might shun evil and choose good.

When Faustus in the play asks the key Simonian question 'Who made the world?' he gives himself the orthodox answer, 'Think Faustus, upon God, that made the world.' Yet there remains much in the play to recall the precepts and temper of Simon's thought. For Faustus and for Simon the most divine knowledge is of the remote order of the heavens and it brings privileges of earthly power exempt from the rule of moral and natural law. For both, magic wins emancipation from the commandments: 'I shall exhibit abundance of gold,' says Simon, 'and shall make and unmake things. I shall be worshipped as God.'

The play's rhetoric of wonder, space and flight may be called Simonian, and the strange conjunctions of nostalgic aspiration with arrogant terrestial ambition that characterise the thought of Simon are to be found also in *Tamburlaine* and *Dr. Faustus*. But the same might be said of Giordano Bruno and of many another Renaissance figure. Marlowe did not need to know the *Recognitions* to recover from the Faust-book the spirit of its first begetter.

The strangest of the Simonian survivals is the apotheosis of Helen. The Faust-book retains only a debased version in which 'the faire *Helena*' is made a 'common concubine and bedfellow', but Marlowe endows her with something like the sanctity that Simon once claimed for her. St. Irenaeus tells us that Simon taught that an 'Understanding leaping forth' from God (i.e. Simon himself) originally went down to the 'lower parts' and produced the powers who made the world; the powers, not liking to be the progeny of another, shut up this 'first thought' in a woman's body and age after age compelled her to move 'as it were from vessel to vessel into other bodies of women'; she passed through the body of Helen of Troy and eventually became a 'common woman' in Tyre, where Simon found and redeemed her.

There is no need to believe Marlowe acquainted with Irenaeus or with another account of Simon and Helen (in the *Recognitions* the paramour is called 'Luna'), but there is a certain consonance of vision. Marlowe brought to the Faust-book a knowledge of classical tributes to Helen and an experience of writing the love-poetry of *Tamburlaine* and *Dido*, and the 'divinity' of the play's Helen is conferred by the presumption of eternity in romantic love and by the immortalising art of the poet.

For the Christian, both Simonian and Faustian myth exhibit the punishment of man for trying through the proud exercise of forbidden knowledge to transcend the bounds of his nature and oppose himself to the laws of creation. For the Simonian, both show the heroic feats of learned magicians who challenge the creator, find in a re-incarnated Helen the prospect of redemption and meet defeat from envious powers determined to keep man in subjection and frustrate his flight to God.

Much has been written about the sources of the *Faustbuch* which might not have been written had not Marlowe and Goethe brought it from the periphery of European literature to its centre. Yet the sources are interesting because they show the shaping of the story by the popular imagination out of comparatively esoteric material.

There are many allusions to an actual early-sixteenth-century Faustus, representing him as a disreputable charlatan, and as with Simon, we cannot be sure that all point to the same figure. A 'Johannes Faust' took a divinity degree at Heidelberg in 1509. But two years earlier the Abbot of Würzburg had warned a friend against a 'Georgius Sabellicus, Faustus iunior', whom he calls necromancer, astrologer and magus secundus'. It appears that this Sabellicus took the name Faustus from the Clementine *Homilies*, in which Clement's father, also a 'Faustus', startles his sons by appearing to them in the shape of Simon Magus. Melanchthon tells of a 'John Faust of Knütlingen' two stories which turn up in the Faust-books and the play—his conjuring of grapes in winter and the attempt made by an old man to convert him. The story of Faustus's death is told in admonitory style by Johann Gast in 1548, and he is the first to hint at the compact with the devil. From other accounts it seems that an historical Faustus died of strychnine poisoning, which leaves the body twisted and deformed—a circumstance which allowed writers to dwell on the grotesque savagery of the devil's exactment of his fee.

The compact with the devil owes most to the sixth-century story of Theophilus of Syracuse. Unjustly deprived of his archdeaconship, he was reputed to have sold himself to the devil by signing a compact in his own blood and forswearing God and the saints; but as he did not repudiate the Virgin he was at last saved by her intercession. A play on the theme was written in the tenth century by the nun Hrotsvitha, with a disaffected soldier substituted for the archdeacon. The *Faustbuch* compact may come from one of several German versions of the Theophilus story.

Another anticipation of Faustus is the legend of St. Cyprian, who was said to have procured a virgin for a nobleman by the assistance of a demon. The Spanish play *El Mágico Prodigioso*, by Calderón (1600-81), was grounded on the Cyprian story and has been contrasted with *Dr. Faustus*. Its hero repents of his sinful magic, suffers martyrdom in the Christian cause and ascends to heaven.

Marlowe was hardly free to offer a repentant Faustus; the power of the story is largely in its hero's incapacity for repentance. Yet like Faustus, the Simon of the New Testament tries to repent, and his last words foreshadow some of the play's: 'Pray ye to the Lord for me, that none of these things which ye have spoken come upon me' (*Acts* viii. 24).

Marlowe, St. Augustine and Faustus of the Manichees

Simon believed that the powers who created the world were hostile to God and contested His dominion over man and creation; he was therefore a *dualist*, seeing a continuing conflict between enduring powers of Good and Evil. To take this view it was necessary to re-interpret Scripture in a special light; Simon claimed this superior knowledge of spiritual things and was therefore a *Gnostic*.

Early Christian theologians were largely concerned with meeting the challenge of the many varieties of Gnostic dualism which flourished in the first four centuries A.D. The problem was to reconcile belief in an omnipotent and omniscient God with the existence of evil in the world he had created. Since *Dr. Faustus* moves in this territory of thought, it often expresses attitudes and ideas cogently formulated in this period. In particular, it harks back to St. Augustine (354-430), from whose work it has proved convenient to illustrate the 'orthodoxy' of some elements of the play. Augustine began as an adherent of Manicheism, one of the most extreme of the Gnostic-dualist sects; and his thought was largely shaped by the way in which he engaged with it and broke free from it.[1] A brief notice of the issues at stake will prevent us from assuming that Marlowe could take for granted a simple opposition between 'Satanism' and 'Christianity'; to believe in such a choice of attitudes is itself a form of dualism, and some modern interpretations of the play (e.g. Ellis-Fermor's) are inadvertently Manichean.

The Manichees taught that the Father of Light and the Prince of Dark-

[1] References to St Augustine's *Confessions* and *City of God* give chapter and paragraph numbers in the Everyman editions. For the Manichees see J. J. O'Meara, *The Young Augustine* (1954), to which this section is indebted.

ness have always existed and the unresolvable conflict between them produced the world and man as we know them. In a fantastic fable they represent the Word of the Father doing battle with the Prince of Darkness and persuading him to swallow a bait of elements—light, water, wind, fire and air. Imprisoned Light has since struggled to escape from Darkness and so bring the world (a mixture of the two) to an end. Salvation is therefore disengagement from the world, the flesh and the devil; and to achieve it man must abstain from worldly affairs, meat, sexual relations and violence.

This may seem remote from *Dr. Faustus*, but it is interesting that Greg gives a Manichean rendering of the lines: 'when all the world dissolves And every creature shall be purified All places shall be hell that is not heaven'. 'Every created thing,' he says, 'shall in the end be *purified* in the sense that it will be no longer mixed, but of one essence, either wholly good or wholly evil.' Augustine would have been more alarmed by the scholar's paraphrase than by the devil's poetry, since for him there can be 'no essence contrary to God'.

The Manicheans found in the nature of man a repetition of the cosmic conflict. Man has two souls: the good soul is divine and of itself can do no evil, but driven by the evil soul of the flesh and the devil, it does what it would not do. Faustus in the play takes a Manichean view: 'The god thou servest is thine own appetite, Wherein is fixed the love of Beelzebub.' But he fails to make the good Manichean choice of an abstemious life, as he sees himself driven by appetite and the devil. The Good and Bad Angels may be held to externalise Faustus's good and evil souls, but not without qualification, since the Bad has no power over the Good Angel; and as we shall see, it is possible to give a quite different account of the angels.

Augustine did not find it easy to distinguish Manichean and Christian attitudes, particularly as both appeal to the New Testament (e.g. *Rom.* vii-viii). But if the distinctions are not made it is hard to escape the view that the world and the flesh are wholly evil and the creator of them cruel, muddled and inefficient. The Manichees held that Christ came to destroy the Old Testament not to fulfil it. To vindicate the integrity of the Bible and to account for evil in creation, Augustine taught that evil is attributable to the abuse of freedom. The will is not inherently evil, but it becomes so when it chooses to prefer lesser to superior good. Evil has no essential existence, but is a deprivation of good; it is the tendency towards none-being which grows stronger as the will falls away from its proper divine objects. Both the fall of man and the fall of the angels came about through a perverse choice of the free will, and each leads to a total negation of all good, both the superior good of heaven and the inferior good of earth. No good, superior or inferior, can be enjoyed unless the will is devoted to God, while the devout will enjoy all modes of good in their due order.

It happens, curiously, that Augustine's principal antagonist in early life was 'a certain Bishop of Manichees whose name was Faustus'. Did Marlowe have this Faustus in mind too? Among other works of Augustine, he might have known his piece 'Against Faustus', which, since it is discussed by Richard Hooker, seems to have had some currency in Elizabethan England. But it is not necessary to treat Augustine's work as source-material in order to see its relevance to the play. The Reformation renewed general interest in Augustine, and among the works helping to disseminate his ideas was at least one that Marlowe seems to have read—*The French Academy* of Peter de la Primaudaye. The references to Augustine offered in the next chapter are meant as a guide to a mode of thought rather than as pointers to Marlowe's reading.

It is often salutary, too, to recall some of the suggestive resemblances between Marlowe and Augustine. Both were proud and preoccupied with pride; skilled in rhetoric yet aware of its seductive power; fascinated by the divinity of man's aspiration but appalled by the perversity of his will. Both began as sceptical critics of the Bible and both 'longed with an incredibly burning desire for an immortality of wisdom' (*Confessions*, III. 7).

Dr. Faustus *and the Bible*

Many of the plays connections with orthodox and heterodox traditions alike may be accounted for by assuming that Marlowe brought his own critical intelligence to bear on certain key passages of the Bible; but he was a trained divinity student with a keen and informed interest in the problems of Biblical interpretation. The detail is best explored through the text of the play, but we do well to remember that Marlowe could expect his audience to be familiar with what the Bible says about Satan as adversary, accuser and prince of this world, about damnation and eternal torment, the temptation and fall of man, and the temptation of Christ in the wilderness. Popular knowledge of these passages would have been pious, but Marlowe's more critical.

The only direct quotations from the Bible in *Dr. Faustus* are from St. Jerome's Latin version, the Vulgate. Rather than take up space with discussion of the English versions Marlowe might have used, I have quoted from one he could not have used—the familiar and convenient Authorised King James version, and where close verbal echoes seem to be suggested it must be remembered that they could equally be supplied from earlier translations or even from the Latin.

Marlowe and The Conflict of Conscience

The Conflict of Conscience is the title of a play by Nathaniel Woods, printed in 1581. But it also serves as a general label for the Protestant literature of conscience with which Miss Lily B. Campbell and others have associated *Dr. Faustus*.[1] In this connection the play may seem to have less to do with the perennial problems of Christianity than with the specific issues of the Reformation.

The Faust-book is a Protestant pamphlet, not only because its Lutheran compiler put in a lot of anti-papist matter but also because it distances the intercessionary agencies of the Church and lets Faustus come personally to terms with God and the devil. *The Conflict of Conscience* is yet more emphatically Protestant, for it is based on the life and death of Francis Spira, who sins by submitting not to the devil but to the devilish Church of Rome. Spira twice recanted his Protestant beliefs under duress from Rome, and his recantation is in Woods's play what the compact with the devil is in Marlowe's. At the crisis of his second recantation the play's hero meets Horror (sent from God) and begins an ordeal of conscience which he endures alone despite the help and sound theological advice of his friends. He prays to God, but his heart is not in it; he despairs and gives himself up for lost; but a messenger reports that he repented truly at the last and died happily.

Woods calls his hero 'Philologus' ('a lover of learning'), but his knowledge is not the sort that 'puffeth up', nor is it a dangerous curiosity. It is a knowledge of God's truth and of the way of salvation. Philologus's tragedy is that he is unable to follow the way that he knows. There is a strong Calvinistic strain in the Spira story, and Calvin himself wrote a preface to one version; and it appears until the last moment that

[1] See L. B. Campbell, 'Dr Faustus: a Case of Conscience', PMLA 67, 1952. *The Conflict of Conscience* is in W. C. Hazlitt, *Dodsley's Old English Plays* (1874) vol. VI.

Philologus is right to feel that he is not among the Elect to whom it is granted to receive Grace, but among the Reprobate pre-destined to damnation.

A number of striking verbal parallels suggest that Marlowe knew either the play or a prose account of Spira's fate. But it does not follow that we must emphasise only the elements shared by *Dr. Faustus* with Spira literature (as Miss Campbell does). There are several ways of treating a conflict of conscience, and Marlowe's is not one of the more naïve ones. Woods's play shows how easy it is for a simple dramatisation of the workings of conscience to become Manichean. Philologus's yielding to temptation is so hard to separate from his delight in the things of this world that it is impossible to feel that pleasure in the created world can be reconciled with godliness of life. The figure of Conscience interprets St. Paul with a Manichean bias: 'We are but strangers all from God, while in this world we dwell.' And Philologus is a simple dualist: 'Sin from the flesh proceeds, but we are of the spirit', and 'the flesh always against the spirit do war'. He dies by refusing food, and his salvation is liberation from a world in which he has been a prey to Tyranny, Hypocrisy, Avarice and Sensual Suggestion.

A quite different approach may be glimpsed in an earlier play, *The World and the Child*,[1] where Conscience speaks for the orderly government of worldly desires not for their total renunciation: 'All mirth in measure is good for thee: But, sir, measure is in all thing.' The classical principle of 'measure' could hardly be insinuated into Woods's play without implying that the good man can be bad within limits—that the soul can compromise with the evil world.

Marlowe in comparison is distinctly Augustinian. Augustine blamed himself for 'accusing the flesh' of the sins for which his will was responsible (*Confessions* IV. 26) and repudiated those who said 'The cause of thy sin is determined in heaven' (*Confessions*, IV. 4). Philologus and Faustus make similar claims, but Wood upholds them while Marlowe does not. When Faustus blames the stars, the flesh and the devil we are made to feel he is excusing a wilful choice. And it is a choice made by Faustus's whole soul. 'Where one deliberates,' says Augustine, 'one soul fluctuates between contrary wills', and the conflict is not 'between two contrary souls, of two contrary substances, from two contrary principles, one good, and the other bad.' (*Confessions*, VIII. 24-25). Again, a distinction

---

[1] *The World and the Child* is in Hazlitt's *Dodsley*, vol. I.

B

which may seem faint or verbal is of immense importance. The dualist
view of two conflicting wills in one man implies that to be good a man
must sever himself from half his own nature. The Augustinian view of
salvation suggests a re-orientation of the whole undivided soul; and it
promises order and delight in this world as well as the next. We shall
find these considerations important when we discuss the conflict pre-
sented in the play.

Sixteenth-century accounts of conscience tell us that the ordeal of fear
is ordained by God, and while it is experienced there is still hope. But
the wilful man may continue to dismiss his fears until his heart is hardened and he loses in the terrors of despair his capacity for contrition and
repentance. Macbeth cries that he has 'supped full of horrors', and
Philologus that 'Confusion is always before my face'; both suffer the
'false illusion' that Theologius in the earlier play attributes to a 'mind
corrupted'; but Macbeth, habituated to fear and ultimately indifferent
to it, is in worse state than Philologus, who turns in his distress 'unto the
spirit of truth' and at last casts out 'all horror and confusion'. Macbeth's
very virtue of courage is perversely displayed in his war against moral
horror. Brutus, in *Julius Caesar*, tells how 'Between the acting of a dread-
ful thing And the first motion, all the interim is Like a phantasma or a
hideous dream'. Macbeth, at first tormented in such interims, contrives
at last to close them when he makes the 'firstlings of his heart' the 'firstlings of his hand'. Elizabethan prose offers many eloquent passages on
conscience, among them several in the *French Academy* which Marlowe
might have known; of the conscience-stricken, it says: God 'terrifieth
them also by dreames and maketh them to tremble at their owne
fancies'.

Dr. Faustus invites discussion in these terms too. Faustus hardens his
heart by resolutely dismissing the salutary fears of conscience. He sins
against the Holy Spirit and despairs. Or could it be that God hardens
his heart, as he hardened the heart of Pharaoh? or might it be the devil,
the Satan who 'entered into' Judas Iscariot?

Dr. Faustus *and the Morality Play*

The ties of *Dr. Faustus* with medieval drama are more easily recognised
than traced. It is impossible (even were it useful) to say how the Seven
Deadly Sins or the Good and Bad Angels reached Marlowe from *The
Castle of Perseverance* or from *Mary Magdalene*, and hard to know what

to make of the mixing of farce with solemnities about despair and grace in the play *Mankind* which 'anticipates' Marlowe by over a hundred years.[1] But we can read the extant Moralities for the impression they give of the moral entertainments still current in Marlowe's time, and for what they reveal of the reaction of dramatic modes of expression on traditional modes of thought. It is particularly important to notice what they make of the devil, of temptation and of forbidden knowledge.

Bishop Bale's *The Temptation of Our Lord* (1538) is one of the best examples, and it betrays the tension between medieval and Renaissance attitudes that is brought to a crisis in *Dr. Faustus.* Although Christ is its hero, Bale writes his most convincing heroic style when he speaks for Satan the Tempter:

Lo, how say ye now; is not here a pleasant sight?
If ye will, ye may have here all the world's delight.
Here is to be seen the kingdom of Arabia;
With all the regions of Afric, Europe and Asia;
And their whole delights, their pomp, their magnificence,
Their riches, their honour, their wealth, their concupiscence.
Here is gold and silver in wonderful habundance. ...

and so on, through 'silks, velvets, tissues', 'fair women', 'camels', 'stout horses' and 'so many pleasures that your heart can desire'. The devil's eloquence is much more celebrative than it is in most medieval plays. Bale is careful not to represent the 'world's delight' as evil and he makes Jesus answer:

Well, He be praised which is of them the giver.

The playwright's own pleasure in the things of this world witnesses, like the Midsummer Shows and civic pageantry, to the Tudor discovery of the bountiful splendours of the earth.

Bale's play may also remind us that Miracle and Morality plays offered two versions of the devil. One is heroic—the defiant Lucifer contesting the throne of God or claiming dominion over the world; the other,

[1] Versions of the earlier plays mentioned here, including *Wyt and Science*, are in J. Q. Adams (ed.), *Chief Pre-Shakespearean Dramas* (1924). The Bale quotation is from J. S. Farmer (ed.), *The Dramatic Writings of John Bale* (1907). *The Four Elements, Lusty Juventus* and *The Marriage of Wit and Science* are in Hazlitt's *Dodsley*, vols. I and II.

unheroic and comic—Satan down on his luck and trying to get his own back somehow. An early instance is the North Town *Fall of Lucifer*; at one point Lucifer occupies the throne of God and 'Above sunne and mone and sterrys on high' commands the reverence of angels and men; but the moments he tumbles from Heaven he becomes a comic figure bent on blowing out the fire of hell with his own wind. Later diabolical figures are apt to keep both the heroic and the unheroic qualities of the devil. Bale's Satan follows up his heroic appeal to Christ with this squalid one:

> Forsake the belief that ye have in God's word,
> That ye are His son, for it is not worth a turd.

Bale was not afraid of precipitous clashes between the high and low, reverent and blasphemous, spiritual and animal. Nor was Marlowe.

An interest in knowledge, study, wit and science is more characteristic of the later Moralities and has only modest medieval beginnings. But distinctions which first become conspicuous in Tudor drama had long been made in theological and homiletic writing. When Eve tasted the fruit of the Tree of Knowledge her sin was not only disobedience but also curiosity. Curiosity is sometimes treated as an intellectual vice, but since the fall brought shame into the world, it is associated too with concupiscence. Thus in *Mary Magdalene*, Curiosity is represented as a seducer and a gallant. The medieval playwrights feared the wayward flesh more than the wayward intellect. The figure of Knowledge in *Everyman* represents a simple uncomplicated knowledge of the doctrines and rites of the Church; by way of confession, penance, contrition, the sacraments and extreme unction, he conducts the hero to salvation.

A number of complexities are introduced, however, by the didactic playwrights of the sixteenth century. *Lusty Juventus (c. 1550)* makes Knowledge represent 'True Knowledge of God's Verity', but now with a Protestant bias supported by extensive Biblical quotations; this is the sort of knowledge that Philologus has in *The Conflict of Conscience*. In other plays we are made more aware of the Renaissance than of the Reformation. The remarkable *Interlude of the Four Elements (c. 1519)* offers its audience an austere education in 'all subtle science' culled from 'cunning Latin books'. Studious Desire and other fittingly named characters explain to Humanity the properties of the four elements, the shape and size of the universe, 'certain points of cosmography' and a

variety of meteorological phenomena. Humanity is exhorted 'more
science to acquire. For the more that thou desirest to know anything,
Therein thou seemest the more a man to be.' Man is distinguished from
the beasts by his knowledge, and through a refined knowledge of God's
creation he comes to knowledge of God Himself. The enemies of
Studious Desire and Experience (a much-travelled character) are Sensual
Appetite, a Taverner and (displacing the devil in importance) 'the rude
beast Ignorance'.

   Dr. Faustus, in relation to these plays, might be called both a medieval
and a Renaissance Morality; but it challenges and displaces the simple
oppositions of earlier plays: 'subtle science' and 'Studious Desire" become the begetters of 'Sensual Appetite' and the devil is credited with
an impressive 'Knowledge of God's Verity'. Yet it retains the great rival
simplicities; from the one side, a continuing reverence for the moral
processes of God's justice; and from the other, a continuing delight in
knowledge of the created world.

   Another 'Renaissance Morality', John Redford's *Wyt and Science*
(*c.* 1530), tells of the courtship between Wit, a student, and Lady
Science, daughter of Reason and Experience. In spite of the antics of
Idleness, Ignorance and other enemies of learning, the comedy accom-
plishes the marriage and so sets the faculties of the studious mind in good
order, even allowing a place for 'Honest Recreation'. Science warns her
bridegroom that she is like most women:

> If ye use me well, in a good sort,
> Then shall I be your joy and comfort;
> But if ye use me not well, then dowt me
> For, sure, ye were better then without me!

The play's dominant moral is human rather than religious, but it is said
at last that Science is 'God's gift' to be used 'Unto God's honour, and
profit both Of you and your neighbour'. The point that Science should
profit mankind and the commonweal is also made in a later play on the
same theme, *The Marriage of Wit and Science* (*c.* 1570). This version
significantly names its most recalcitrant character 'Will' and makes him
the greatest obstruction to the modest and serviceable partnership of
Wit and Science. Dr. Faustus, in a less naïve way, is diverted from
service by the seductive power of the will.

   Dr. Faustus cannot, however, reach the comic solutions of the *Wit and*

Science plays with their assurance that once the proper relationships are established, mankind will live happily ever after. Marlowe brings to the material of the later Moralities the preoccupation with man under sentence of death that is characteristic of the early Moralities. This does not mean that he set out to combine two kinds of play. It is enough to suppose that he understood and perhaps shared, the misgivings that Christians were apt to have about the claims of advancing knowledge. De la Primaudaye writes, for example, 'Of Curiosity and Novelty':

> The ill success of our age affordeth us too many miserable testimonies, wherein at this day we see nothing but contrarieties of opinions and uncertainties, through their subtilties and bold curiosities, who have sought to pluck (as a man would say) out of heaven the secrets hid from the Angels; yea, which is worse, have boasted that they have attained unto the knowledge of them, filling our times with trouble and confusion under that false pretence.

Elsewhere, in the course of a discussion of meteorology, he censures those

> who are esteemed very learned in Natural Philosophy, and in all other letters and human sciences; who are so badly advanced in the knowledge of God by them, that instead of acknowledging and glorifying him as it behooveth them, they rather become Atheists and Epicures, contemners and mockers of his Majestie, and of all religion.[1]

Marlowe himself enjoyed a reputation as 'Atheist and Epicure', contemner and mocker of religion. Thomas Kyd and Richard Baines, under pressure from the authorities, brought against him many charges of blasphemy, heresy and atheism. He was accused, for instance, of saying 'that the first beginning of Religioun was only to keep men in awe', and 'that Moyses was a Jugler and Aaron a cosener the one for his miracles to Pharao to prove there was a god, & the other for takeing the eareringes of the children of Israell to make a golden calfe'. Other reported sayings are yet more critical and truculent; and it seems that Marlowe delivered a lecture in defence of atheism and perhaps started on an atheistical treatise. There is no need to gloss over these charges. We may admit them as true while abstaining from the conclusion that Marlowe was in-

[1] Quotations from De la Primaudaye's *French Academy* are from the first complete English edition, of 1618.

capable of reverence or of a serious evaluation of Christianity. His sceptical and rebellious temperament was not simply 'his personal tendency'; it made him (like Giordano Bruno) one of the great representative figures of his time, capable of the fullest experience of the intellectual and moral ordeals of his generation.

Marlowe and Heroic Tragedy

Dr. Faustus is both the consummation of the English Morality tradition and the last and finest of Marlowe's heroic plays. As a Morality it vindicates humility, faith and obedience to the law of God; as an heroic play it celebrates power, beauty, riches and knowledge, and seems a sequel to the plays of *Tamburlaine the Great*.

Tamburlaine is more often regarded as the start of a tradition than as the end of one. Yet it has its past in the history of popular entertainment, and we must take note of it if we are fully to understand the heroic element in *Dr. Faustus*. In glancing at Bale's *Temptation of Our Lord* we noticed that Satan's appeal to Christ owed something to Bale's delight in the pomp and splendour of civic pageantry. The traditions of public spectacle are yet more precisely and conspicuously behind the plays of *Tamburlaine*. The records of Midsummer and Lord Mayor's Shows prove that Africa and the Mediterranean had a special place in the Tudor imagination long before the writing of *Tamburlaine* and *Othello*. From the beginning of the sixteenth century a King of Moors had played a part in civic spectacle and helped to enrich the public's conception of power, riches and sensual splendour. His practical function may have been to clear a way for the religious and civic shows that followed. But the King of Moors or the Sultan (sometimes we find both) seems to have overawed the crowd, not bullied them. He was expensively got up, in red satin and silver paper, mounted on horse-back under a pavillion carried by attendants, and set at the head of a procession of slaves and concubines.[1]

Marlowe owes the form of *Tamburlaine* to processional pageant, as the stage-directions constantly remind us:

> Tamburlaine leading Zenocrate: Techelles, Usumcasane, and other lords and soldiers, loaden with treasure. (197)

[1] For the King of the Moors in pageant, see Malone Society, *Collections Vol. III*, ed. Jean Robertson and D. J. Gordon.

The Banquet: and to it cometh Tamburlaine all in scarlet, Zenocrate,
Theridamas, Techelles, Usumcasane, the Turk, Bajazeth in his cage,
Zabina, with others. (1638)

Even the cage is a pageant property. But the true magnificence of Marlowe's achievement is not the telling of the story by passing from one
great show to another. It is rather in his transmutation of spectacle into
word:

> Go, stout Theridamas! thy words are swords. (82)

Here is one of the many sustained passages of verbal pageantry:

> A hundred Tartars shall attend on thee,
> Mounted on steeds swifter than Pegasus;
> Thy garments shall be made of Median silk,
> Enchas'd with precious jewels of mine own,
> More rich and valorous than Zenocrate's.
> With milk-white harts upon an ivory sled,
> Thou shalt be drawn amidst the frozen pools (289 *ff*)

These opulent and decorative hyperboles may owe something to
Spenser—another pageant poet who transformed civic spectacle into
word. But Spenser was more aware of the moral allegory of pageant,
Marlowe of its exotic dreams of wealth and empire. The language of
Tamburlaine reaches beyond the resources of pageant inventory—the
silver paper, dummy lances and fireworks; but it reaches in the same
direction—towards the glorification of earthly sovereignty. It is not 'rant
and youthful crudity' but the declamation of an innocent imperialism.
The sublimated, optimistic, violent humanism of the early Marlowe
springs from the accord of his temperament with the mood of his time.
His elder imitators, Peele and Greene, could not bend his bow, but it was
not for want of trying. Marlowe, in his precocious maturity, was the
first to outgrow the adolescent dreams of *Tamburlaine*. When he turned
from the exotic material of Scythian conquest to the homelier pages of
the chronicles from which he made *Edward II* he set aside his magnificent
toy trumpet.

When he took it up again in *Dr. Faustus* he sounded it to different purpose. Much of Tamburlaine's heroical hyperbole belongs to his role as
'the scourge of God'; but when Valdes and Cornelius use similar 'high

astounding terms' to Faustus they are the agents of the devil—tempters like Bale's Satan. In *Dr. Faustus* heroic verse must come to terms with the Christian order.

Tamburlaine is not only about terrestial glory, however. It owes its imaginative unity to its cosmography and to its treatment of the four elements. Michael Drayton said of Marlowe that his 'raptures were all air and fire, which made his verses clear'. This felicity is apt in a quite technical sense. Air and Fire were respectively the 'hot and moist' and 'hot and dry' elements whose peculiar property was to ascend upwards in a straight line. Marlowe in *Tamburlaine* fashions poetry, character and spectacle from air and fire, finally transmuting all into pure fire. Fire is associated with 'choler' and air with 'blood'; 'bloody and insatiate Tamburlaine' is 'a fiery thirster after sovereignty'. His enemies are without fire and afflicted with the cold humours of phlegm and melancholy; Cosroe, for example, is 'gross and like the massy earth That moves not upwards'. In Part II it is said of Tamburlaine's sons that 'Water and air being symbolised in one Argue their want of courage and of wit'. The King of Soria hopes that Tamburlaine's heart will 'Dry up with anger and consume with heat'. But a friend makes a virtue of the same fiery end, 'sooner let the fiery element Dissolve and make your kingdom in the sky, Than this base earth should shroud your majesty'.

It is, then, entirely apt that fire should be a feature of the spectacle. The hearse of Zenocrate is carried across the stage with 'the drums sounding a doleful march; the town burning', and Tamburlaine's speech turns spectacle into word—'Flame to the highest regions of the air And kindle heaps of exhalations'. In the last scene the hearse of Zenocrate is brought to 'serve as parcel in the funeral' of Tamburlaine, and it is possible that the final spectacle was of a funeral pyre, giving literal point to the last choric lines:

> For earth hath spent the pride of all her fruit
> And heaven consumed her choicest living fire (4643-4)

Tamburlaine dies a victim to the mere processes of mutability, but there is consolation in the feeling that his soul dissolves in the aspiring elements, his flesh being 'not of force enough, To hold the fiery spirit it containes'.

Among the possible sources of *Tamburlaine* has been counted de la Primaudaye's *French Academy*. It offers a full discussion of the four elements and the astronomical order, which Marlowe may have consulted for his first play and to which he may have returned for his last. Both Tamburlaine and Faustus are the heroes of cosmic plays, their aspirations not confined to the earth that they embrace; but one is consumed by the fire of Heaven and the other by the fire of Hell.

Marlowe's heroic tragedy may also be claimed to have classical antecedents. The death of Tamburlaine recalls the destruction and purification by fire of the hero in Seneca's *Hercules Oetaeus*; while the conjurations, flying chariots and apparitions of *Dr. Faustus* have dramatic precedents in Seneca's *Medea*. More important than the specific debts, however, is Marlowe's re-discovery of certain of the great antique themes of tragedy. Greek tragedy, from its beginning, is much concerned with the boundaries set to the pride and accomplishment of man; with his mistaking his little life for the whole of life and his limited power for omnipotence. It does not make an exultant delight in life and a full exercise of human power culpable in themselves—without them there could be no heroes. But when a more than common human virtue mistakes itself for super-human virtue, it challenges divine wrath and its presumption or *hubris* is fittingly punished and rewarded. It is perhaps the central mystery of tragedy that the pride which makes the hero also destroys him. Marlowe, sensitive to his Christian and Humanist inheritances alike, learned to make the same point with something like the Greek clarity and ritual intensity. *Tamburlaine* and *Dr. Faustus* both celebrate the aspirations and the power of man; the presumption of the one is checked by death, 'the Monarke of the earth', and the presumption of the other meets 'the heavy wrath of God'.

Heroic Morality and The Jew of Malta

If *The Jew of Malta* was indeed the earlier play, then it anticipated the assimilation of heroic tragedy into Morality that is accomplished in *Dr. Faustus*. Marlowe's blasphemy, as T. S. Eliot reminds us, is of a piece with his Christianity. And this is manifestly true of his perverse and topsy-turvy Morality, *The Jew of Malta*. It is a ruthless travesty of both Christian and Atheist moral orders. Here, in place of the formal Christian Chorus, Machiavelli appears and speaks a new version of the Law; and just as the Chorus of *Faustus* will disclose the hero in his study, so Old Nick shows us Barabas (significantly named) in his counting-house.

Through the rest of the play, the kingdom, the power and the glory belong not to God, but to the caricatured Machiavelli and to the hero who honours his laws. Barabas only becomes master of the plot when he abdicates his glowing heroic ambitions and sets about the nasty intrigues which he conducts like a Morality devil, exploiting hypocrisy, treachery and a range of human frailties which in the old plays would have been personified as the devil's henchmen.

The Kingdom is purchased by treachery and sold by deceit—the kingly 'trades'. Power is not the exercise of strength and courage but of blackmail and treason, and the powerful are not the soldiers but the poisoners and seducers. Glory ceases to belong to the magical splendours of an earthly crown and to earth's bounty of precious stones, and lurks in the crown-coins that the 'shagrag' knaves of Malta clutch from one another. And where Helen and Zenocrate inspire in other plays a sensuality of almost saving purity, the heroine here is Bellamira, a prostitute down on her luck.

Once the Prologue's creed of 'no sin but ignorance' and 'religion is but a childish toy' is accepted, the Jew Barabas can be seen as a tragic hero, and he remains heroic as long as he advances himself by insight and practical skill. But his fall comes through two tragic errors: the first a failure of skill, 'One dram of powder more had made all sure'; and the second a failure of insight—he entrusts the Christian Ferneze with a knife. Both failures might be attributed to the atheistical equivalent of the sin of pride—over-confidence. On the basis of its declared morality, the play is the tragedy that the Prologue holds it to be. But, of course, the declared morality is manifestly outrageous. 'Assume the Prologue is right,' Marlowe seems to say, 'and build a tragic morality on its system—it turns into this grotesque absurdity.' T. S. Eliot has called the play a farce. It is a very trenchant one.

It ends becomingly with the 'damnation' of the hero when he falls through his own man-trap and is discovered in a fiery cauldron. He dies cursing as the 'extremity of heat' pinches him with 'intolerable pangs', a martyr to the Prologue's faith.

Marlowe in *The Jew of Malta* shows a moral and intellectual courage challenging Christian and anti-Christian thought alike. His very truculence has a purging power; but it spares nothing—least of all the heroic values that inspired the early poetry. The joke is played at the expense of Christian Morality, Atheist Morality and Heroic Tragedy; but the demolition prepares the ground for a finer monument to all three.

Marlowe and Renaissance Italy

Marlowe would have been less ready to look beyond conventional horizons had he not been stirred by the flight of Italian art and speculation. *Dr. Faustus*, although without specific Italian sources, owes its audacity of thought and temper to Renaissance Italy, and treats with a comparable reach of mind questions that troubled Italian thinkers from Petrarch to Giordano Bruno. Marlowe's affinities with Italy are too multiple and various to be reviewed in small space. But to get some impression of the Renaissance quality of *Dr. Faustus* it is enough to read three short pieces readily available in translation—Petrarch 'On his Own Ignorance', Lorenzo Valla's 'Dialogue on Free Will' and Pico della Mirandola's 'Oration on the Dignity of Man'.[1] Petrarch reconciles a Renaissance delight in life and learning with an Augustinian recognition of the limitations of man, and a devotion to eloquence with a devotion to dogma. Valla's elegant argument illuminates his theme but leaves its paradoxes as teasing as it finds them, adding a stringent warning against pursuing moral questions too far. Pico, marvellously exemplifying the heroic possibilities of debate, vindicates the *magus* who 'weds earth to heaven' and 'lower things to the endowments and powers of higher things'.

But the Italian who most often anticipates the dynamic and mysterious qualities of Marlowe's intellectual vision is Marsilio Ficino. Ficino shares Marlowe's awareness of the sanctity and torment of desire—'by a natural instinct every soul strives in a continuous effort both to know all truths by the intellect and to enjoy all things by the will'. Through its striving the soul reaches out towards harmony with the cosmic order, and by the exercise of the four *furores* (music and poetry, religious rites, prophecy, and love) man can enjoy the most beneficent influences (flowings-in) from the stars and planets. Whether we treat Ficino's astrological theory of the power of words (*vis verborum*) as fantasy, as naïve science or as valid allegory, we must recognise it as an attempt to explain why eloquence seems often to refresh our moral being even before we are fully alive to its meaning. Marlowe exercises the poetic *furore* without giving an astrological account of it. But his rhetoric often

[1] The Italian texts named are available in English in *The Renaissance Philosophy of Man*, ed. Cassirer, Kristeller and Randall (1948). For an account of the *furores* doctrine, see D. P. Walker, *Spiritual and Demonic Magic from Ficino to Campanella* (1958).

commands imagery of cosmic space, and the verse of *Tamburlaine* is indebted, as we have seen, to Renaissance cosmography. Marlowe's distinction was to make the verbal magic efficacious in English—to put audiences under a spell. His eloquence often endows sweetness with power and power with sweetness in a way that disarms conventional moral judgments. The problem arises in *Dr. Faustus* (as in *Othello* and *Antony and Cleopatra*), for the play does not leave us free to assume uncritically that poetic eloquence is one thing and moral truth quite another. It may be claimed that what we value most at the end is not the piety of the good but the rhetoric of the damned.

2. *The Tragedy of Dr. Faustus*

Transposing the Faustus story into English Morality-play, Marlowe tapped the hidden potentials of both the myth and the dramatic form. From the myth he released energies that had troubled Christendom from the time of Simon Magus, and from the Morality form he wrested the clarity and mystery of tragedy. Both potentials had been concealed by didactic writers who tamed, distanced or ignored the difficulties and challenges of their material. Instead of celebrating the aspiration and revealing the presumption of man, the Faust-books relished the magician's cheek and gloated over his mangled remains; while the Morality-plays, instead of meeting honestly the problem of evil in a divine world, lapsed into Manichean notions of a devil in command of the flesh and its desires.

We may begin by allowing cool moral reflection a little more than its due, and dividing the play into three phases. The first phase, down to the signing of the compact, is Augustinian. Faustus's passion for knowledge and power is in itself a virtue, but diverted from the service of God it threatens to become totally negative and self-destroying. The devil in this phase is not a tempter but a frightening witness to the lack of heroic consolations in the state of damnation, and Faustus's indifference to his warnings is manifest and culpable folly. In human terms, Faustus is a fool to believe that knowledge can be satisfyingly pursued in the service of 'self-conceit'.

The second phase, to the end of the fourth act, is much more am-
biguous. On the one hand, it is almost Simonian in its vindication of
'natural magic', as Mephostophilis now collaborates with Faustus's self-
regarding desires for knowledge, power and sensual satisfaction (or, as
Levin puts it, his *libido sciendi, libido dominandi* and *libido sentiendi*). But,
on the other hand, all these satisfactions prove poor compensation for the
loss of heaven, and Faustus comes to know that he is committed to hell,
to that deprived condition of life in which, before the compact, he had
refused to believe. His moral distress becomes genuine now, but it is
too late: he has committed the sin against the Holy Spirit and, humanly
speaking, has lapsed into habitual egoism.

In the last phase of the play the damnation of Faustus is ruthless and
absolute, the proper punishment of 'self-conceit'. Yet we are made to
feel that it is a reward too—an end at once pitiful and magnificent—with
the experience of damnation endorsing the splendours of the moral
order in a final vision of the wrath and the sacrificial love of God. But
what about the unfortunate Faustus 'being in hell for ever'? The answer
is best reserved to the end.

The Worship of the Devil

A prologue may delay the delighted shock of a leap into theatrical
illusion, lapse into apology or brag, or cheat suspense by betraying the
plot. But this one is an exequy to sweetness and audacity while its tone
assures us that these qualities are still at the poet's command. Even without speculating about the lost play to which the first lines allude, or
wondering if the next refer to *Edward II*, or recognising *Tamburlaine* in
'the pomp of proud audacious deeds', we feel that the heroic tradition is
about to be transcended by one of its masters.

When the pace is checked with an appeal to 'patient judgments' there
is still a play on words ('perform the form'), and while the story is to be
morally momentous, we feel it is to keep the buoyant excitements of
simplicity. We are told that Faustus so profited from his divinity-studies
and so adorned the field of scholarship that he won a doctor's degree and
excelled all others in debate; but the prose-sense is transfigured by the
resonant diction often used in the Renaissance to make scholarship and
theology lyrical and heroic. Yet 'waxen wings' and 'melting' recall the
Icarus story and remind us that dissolution occurs at the highest point of

human flight. Faustus is 'swollen with cunning of a self-conceit', recalling St. Paul's 'Knowledge puffeth up', and it is appropriate to remember that Simon Magus was also often compared with Icarus. But Marlowe retains some sense of the splendour and poignancy of human flight and fall—the wings are vulnerable but they do 'mount' and their melting is 'conspired'. In the Faust-book, Faustus 'taking to himself the wings of an eagle, thought to flie over the whole world' and Marlowe's Dido cries for 'wings of waxe like Icarus' (*Dido*, 1651); and Renaissance art and speculation were often, as with Leonardo, fascinated by the prospect of flying.

Like Lucifer in the old plays, however, Faustus ceases to be heroic once he has fallen. As in so much devil-legend, the angel turns into a beast, and here flight is displaced by gluttony—Faustus is 'glutted' with 'learning's golden gifts' and 'surfeits upon' necromancy. So it comes about that the Prologue's last line admits both awe and contempt for the fallen hero: 'And this the man that in his study sits.'

The First Soliloquy

Faustus's first soliloquy is a second prologue, but the hero's to his own design, not Marlowe's to the play. The formal Prologue brightens the highlights and deepens the shadows of the soliloquy.

Disclosed in his study by the Prologue (or perhaps in view from the start), Faustus may close a book as he says, 'Settle thy studies', or he may mean 'determine the purpose of your studies.' Either way, he means to meditate his choice of profession, and we are astonished that after his promise to 'sound the depths' his soundings so promptly seem quick and shallow, and we are throughout made more aware of his virtuosity in debate than of his gravity as a philosopher. *The French Academy* (I. 4), commenting on 'what men ought chiefly to level at', says the 'art' of Philosophy is 'to find out, and to know the truth both of divine and human things. She teacheth us to adore and serve God, and to love man.' Faustus perverts both divine and human values by asking of each art and knowledge how well it serves his 'self-conceit'.

His rhetoric of renunciation flaunts his mastery of each 'art', reduces it to a limited end and dismisses it by boasting he has attained it. Having graduated, he will be a theologian only 'in show' and devote his whole being to Aristotle. The scholars in the audience would see that he cultivates the new logic based on the 'sweet Analytics' and not the old, based on the *De Interpretatione*, and that his Latin definition of logic is quoted from Aristotle's keenest Renaissance critic, Peter Ramus. But none could mistake his devotion to Aristotle for a mere proper respect, and even those unacquainted with Ramus would be awed by the Latin words, which ring out like a spell before they are translated and contemptuously set aside. When he bids 'on kai me on' farewell, the Greek words ('being and not being') may remind the few that the study of Aristotle has a contemplative end above 'disputing well'.

Faustus finds no place for mere devotion to truth or to the service of God and man. He despises Medicine for only curing the sick, and when he quotes Aristotle on the 'end of physic' he mutilates the argument of the *Ethics* (I. 7) that the purpose of man is 'an activity of the soul in accordance with goodness'. He despises Justinian and the law for being concerned with the just distribution of property, and he reduces service and humility to drudgery and servility. He rejects the human arts not because they 'puff up' but because they do not puff up enough.

But there are qualities in his self-regarding desires that make him something other than a common sinner. The moral shocks he administers are exhilarating as well as disturbing. He is a clear master of the disputant's art he relinquishes, and even when he speaks of 'gold' it seems heroically alluring until it is contemned by an intellectual passion— 'A greater subject fitteth Faustus' wit.' A plague-threatened audience must have been awed at the accomplishment of one whose 'common talk' offered healing prescriptions, and still more awed to find the art despised. The 'universal body of the Law' shrinks to 'A petty case of paltry legacies', a 'servile and illiberal profession'. To our heroic sense these attitudes witness to the infinity of human desire and leave us reluctant to shrivel to life-size.

Faustus returns to Divinity to see if it is the 'best' knowledge to afford great miracles, fit his intellectual powers and exempt him from drudgery. The soliloquy is checked to allow Faustus to take up Jerome's Bible and 'view it well'. When it resumes, the waxen wings of his rhetoric flag as heaven conspires his overthrow—the sombre Latin texts no longer collaborate with the flight of the verse. Unlike the other quotations, these from the Bible have the same force for all, and few would miss the betrayal of Christian doctrine. Faustus amputates both his first text (*Rom.* vi. 23) and his second (1 *Ep. John* i. 8). Had he read on in the first he would have found, 'but the gift of God is eternal life through Jesus Christ our Lord', and in the second, 'If we confess our sins he is faithful and just to forgive us our sins.' But he censures the doctrines of grace, repentance and atonement, comes to rest in the ugliest of the Bible's statements about the plight of man and insists on the human limitations he is trying to transcend. In an earlier Elizabethan work Satan makes a syllogism identical with Faustus's, and a Christian Knight refutes him by appealing from the Law, which condemns man, to the Gospel by which he is redeemed. The same appeal is still open to Christians, but even non-Christians may recognise in the syllogism a disputant's trick and a culpable failure of humility. Faustus wilfully denies himself the choice of salvation. Or so it seems at the time—at the end Mephostophilis will claim to have turned the leaves and led the eyes of Faustus from text to text. So long as Faustus is resolutely committed to the Law without the Gospel, the Law will shape his fortune. By an act of will he makes himself a victim to the doctrine he despises—'what will be shall be', and his 'Divinity, adieu' will have a different meaning at the end of the play.

The moral crisis of the soliloquy does not coincide with the highest reach of its poetry. Marlowe has to recover the flight of Faustus's thought without altogether disarming 'patient judgment'. He insinuates into the rest of the speech two kinds of delight in knowledge and power. First, the childish pleasure in the paraphernalia of magic ('Lines, circles, signs, letters and characters'), shadowed by the Prologue's 'cursed necromancy'; and then the high ambition for intellectual dominion over the spacious cosmos, brightened by the Prologue's 'heavenly matters' and 'heavenly verse'. Profit and delight, power and honour seem at last untainted by terrestial suggestions and seem won not by action but by study. The 'quiet poles' are of the cosmos, not of the earth, and the 'things that move between' include the stars and planets in their courses. Without this image we would still marvel at the dynamic accomplishments within the reach of study; but with it we feel that the mind comes to rest without forfeiting its mastery of motion; 'All things that move between the quiet poles Shall be at my command.' The next lines, making the practical point that kings cannot control the weather, are touched with wonder at the science of meteorology, and 'dominion' becomes an act of thought which 'Stretcheth as far as doth the mind of man'.

Looking back to the earlier line, 'Yet art thou still but Faustus, and a man', we can recognise in it all the pathos and folly, arrogance and

C

...endour of a man bound to the human condition he refuses to accept. Had it ended the soliloquy, the play could hardly have proceeded, but placed at the centre it is not a confession of defeat but an occasion for super-human resolution. We admire the contemplative scholar, but deplore the practising magician who disdains both God and man. In the A-text the magician is 'a mighty god', in the B-text a 'Demi-god' (the first perhaps a reporter's vulgarisation and the second an editorial dilution of a blasphemy), but the last line is unequivocally hubristic—'Here tire my brains to get a deity'. This is the voice of a man with an impossible job on his hands, and again we feel both awe and contempt for the 'cunning of a self-conceit'.

The Fall to Necromancy

The Good and Bad Angels (I. i. 68-75) speak only after the soliloquy has done its work, and their function is to keep the audience's moral perspective clear. The Good offers the moral view of the Prologue and the Bad the heroic and hubristic one of the soliloquy. Like the devil in the wilderness, the Bad offers the power and glory of the world, and Faustus's response (which could be a continuation of his soliloquy) instantly yields to the temptation Christ turned aside.

The moral frame established, Faustus is allowed a fanciful extravaganza (76-96) in which power and glory are brought up to date with allusions to Parma and Antwerp and coloured by Elizabethan imperial sentiment. There are no evil fantasies yet, but suggestions of energy, daring, bounty and beauty sustaining national pride and exuberant pleasure in trade. But the devil, we may remember, did not tempt Christ to tyranny but to the miraculous exercise of the power of empire. When Faustus hopes to resolve ambiguities and master 'strange philosophy' to make the servile spirits fetch him what he pleases, he is proposing in grander style to turn stones into bread and satisfy his appetites, but there is still a hint, to use Augustine's phrase again, of 'an incredibly burning desire for an immortality of wisdom'.

Through the scene, Faustus is dedicated to 'philosophy' but he distorts it by pursuing the Natural part at the cost of the Divine. As *The French Academy* (I. 4) warns us, such study 'oftentimes serveth to content the curiosity of haughty spirits, than to make them better, in so much that sometimes, by speculation, and by vain and frivolous questions, they seek out the natural causes of things so curiously, that in the end they strive to find out another beginning of all things than GOD.'; and there are some 'who being destitute of God's grace by reason of their sins, give themselves to sooth-saying and to seek after sorcerers'. Mephostophilis will later warn Faustus against 'frivolous demands' and refuse to tell him who made the world.

In his address to the sorcerers Valdes and Cornelius, Faustus surrenders his allegiance to Contemplative Science and gives himself to the wrong kind of Active Science—not Moral Science but necromancy. He knows himself responsible for his fall from scholarism to conjuring ('not your words only but mine own fantasy') and in reviewing the thought of his soliloquy ('law and physic are for petty wits') he totally devalues it, despising the virtuosity that once 'Gravelled the pastors of the German church' and envying the 'cunning' of Agrippa, who entertained Europe with the dancing shades of the dead.

Valdes's speech (117-31) is remarkable for its grotesque imagery of empire, and as he gives to commercial and military enterprise the dimensions and essences of dream, we know what it is to be puffed up. The trio will be obeyed by devils as the Spanish by American natives, be attended by German soldiers, big Laplanders and concubines, and have at its disposal the wealth of Italy and the Spanish colonies—but to put it this way is to taste the sediment and miss the wine. The Good Angel might paraphrase 'you will enjoy only the pleasures of empire if you are wilful'; but the Bad, like Valdes, would have it, 'these are your delights if you are resolute'. The word 'resolute', making a virtue of wilfulness, is a key one: 'If learned Faustus will be resolute'.

Cornelius (134-46) tells how Faustus's grounding in astrology, languages and mineralogy fits him for magical performance, the passage from Contemplative to Active Science. Some in the audience would already know that witches had to understand the influence of heavenly bodies, invoke spirits in Latin, Greek and Hebrew, and know the properties of all substances used in their art. Valdes, speaking for the fruits of power, and Cornelius, for the delights of power as the exercise of knowledge, are only amplifying and explaining what Faustus himself has already expressed.

A very human and domestic Faustus has to fit in his conjuring between dinner and bedtime, and the colloquial rashness of the last line, 'This night I'll conjure though I die therefore' is ominous only because we know the issues at stake better than Faustus does.

The Conjuration

Just before the conjuring we glimpse Faustus's state through the eyes of his servant and the scholars. In classical-comedy style the scholars are outwitted by the servant through a travesty of their own pedantry. Yet the moral theme is alive—anxiety about Faustus's spiritual situation becomes the practical question 'How now sirrah, where's thy master?' and Wagner's cheeky reply 'God in heaven knows' is apter than he intends. The patter about '*corpus naturale*' puts lightly the solemn point that Faustus is 'but a man', Wagner's vain triumph mimics his master's, and the supper with the sorcerers is symbolic and sinister.

There are textual and staging problems in the conjuring scene, since the B-text has Faustus approach 'Lucifer and 4 devils' already on the stage. Greg has them enter 'above', but here as in V.ii they may 'ascend from infernal Dis' by mounting through the trapdoor. They may either come out of hiding or enter 'from below' in the course of the incantation.

In the play Faustus studies Roger Bacon and Pietro d'Abano, but in fact Marlowe picked up from a variety of sources a version of witchcraft very different from the historical d'Abano's. Kocher, observing that d'Abano believed conjuring a holy rite, shows that Marlowe falls in with the 'classical tradition and with the orthodox theological doctrine that any kind of conjuring is worship of the Devil'. Faustus uses all the blasphemous techniques attributed to witches by Christians: the prayer and sacrifice to fiends; the magic circle with astrological insignia; the 'anagrammatizing' of 'Jehovah'; the naming of saints; the invocations; and the use of holy water and the sign of the Cross. Several of these practices were also attributed to Raleigh and his circle and may have been known to Marlowe at first hand. The spectacular language of evil which opens the scene is in the tradition of Seneca's *Medea*, which could offer precedent for the gloom, the dwelling on night and murk, the supplication of the gods of Acheron and even the dragon.

The climax is the appearance of Mephostophilis in the shape of a devil. But instead of the engagement with supernatural evil that we might have expected, we get a farcical anti-clerical joke in the manner of Protestant Interlude, as the devil is told to return as a friar. The lapse into farce is a fall from conjuring in its solemn sense to conjuring in its popular sense—the playing of magical tricks. The joke devalues the claim Faustus

makes as he plays it 'I see there's virtue in my heavenly words' and seems
to make mock of the whole rite.

The Voluntary Ascent of Mephostophilis

Mephostophilis is frighteningly indifferent to Faustus's joke, and in
cool, decisive brevities he makes it clear that he is not the pliant creature
Faustus in childish glee took him for. Vainglory confronts damnation
on different terms from those foreseen. Faustus's ambition is sympto-
matically reduced to a fantasy of negation as he solicits the aid of Mephostophilis, 'Be it to make the moon drop from her sphere, Or the ocean
to overwhelm the world'; and he meets the check, 'I am a servant to
great Lucifer And may not follow thee without his leave.' There is no
zest in his interrogation now, but it is searching and intelligent as he
learns that his conjuring is only the accidental cause of the devil's appearance. Kocher shows that Marlowe was acquainted with the orthodox
doctrine of 'voluntary ascent', which attributes the power of witches to
the negative force of their blasphemies and not to the efficacy of their
spells; the devils come of their own will for the offender's 'glorious soul'.

Mephostophilis promptly displaces Faustus as the intellectual centre of
the play. His eloquence sticks to the facts and sheds the airy and fiery
qualities which continue to characterise the fantasies of Faustus. For a
comparably urbane devil, skilled in theology and capable of finesse, we
should have to look outside the English and German traditions to Italy
(to the Florentine poet Luigi Pulci). Yet, unlike Valdes and Cornelius,
he is not a tempter. He comes, as it were, to represent the terms of the
contract offered to Christ: 'If thou therefore wilt worship me, all shall be
thine'; but he offers no prospect of power and glory and Faustus accepts
his terms before they are made explicit. Confronted by the sudden
revelation of the limits of his own power, Faustus does not weigh his
situation, but with an unreflecting leap of the will dedicates himself to
Beelzebub. The impression of wilfulness is strengthened by the steep
contrast between the heady rashness of the man and the moral objectivity
of the devil ('This word "damnation" terrifies not me'). Faustus's eagerness to make a hero of Lucifer is frustrated by a moral analysis which
insists with liturgical authority on the love and omnipotence of God and
on the misery of the defeated angels (75-81). Mephostophilis holds up
a mirror to Faustus's 'aspiring pride and insolence', but Faustus refuses to
look in it and see the fall he is re-enacting. 'The just cause of the bad

angels' misery,' says Augustine, 'is their departure from that High Essence, to turn back upon themselves. ... Which vice, what is it else but pride?' The choice of the self before God, he explains, is caused by the evil of the will, which in itself is inexplicable: 'For what can cause the will's evil, the will being sole cause of all evil?' (*City of God*, XII. vi). Marlowe expresses this doctrine dramatically by making us aware of the perverse momentum of Faustus's will and of the analogue between his state and that of the fallen angels.

But even in human terms Faustus is culpable—he is obstinately indifferent to an intellect and experience manifestly superior to his own. Mephostophilis is dismissed as if he were emissary from a Duke to a King ('Go bear these tidings to great Lucifer'), but Faustus for all his command of manner is only pretending to dictate terms that are of the devil's making; Mephostophilis's compliance is his triumph, and Faustus is left alone to amplify his fantasies of power and glory in consolatory hyperboles.

Faustus's folly is felt most keenly in his bracing scorn of the devil's account of damnation. The stress is here on the mental ordeal of hell, an idea of which Augustine shows us the antiquity:

> Now, as for this worm and this fire, they that make them only mental pains do say that the fire implies the burning in grief and anguish of the soul, that now repents too late for being severed from the sight of God (*City of God*, XXI. ix).

Both Augustine and Marlowe find it possible to see hell as both mental and physical torment, but by putting an early emphasis on the anguish of a too-late repentance, Marlowe brings home to us Faustus's moral insensibility—hell becomes an immanent condition of life to which he is immediately exposed and not a remote prospect to be shrugged off. Mephostophilis's most celebrated line, 'Why this is hell nor am I out of it' makes, as we shall see, an orthodox point about devils carrying torment with them wherever they go; but, spoken from the stage platform to the theatre, its blighted objectivity reminds us that human life itself can be a state of deprivation and pain. Faustus strengthens this impression by talking as if he and Mephostophilis were in the same condition, with the difference that the devil lacks 'manly fortitude', but the devil's insight, suffering and humility betray the shallowness of the man who presumes to teach him about damnation. Faustus ought to have some apprehension of hell, but he has none. Guilty of a terrible complacency, he betrays an incapacity for moral experience which is of a piece with his indifference to the plight of Mephostophilis.

Conflict and Resolution

There are two kinds of conflict in the play: one between rival views of the nature of evil, and the other between the choice of good and the choice of evil. The first is at its sharpest in the contrast in the first acts between Faustus and Mephostophilis; the second, in the play's soliloquies. Faustus's initial obstinacy makes him persist in an heroic view of evil and renders him incapable of moral reflection.

The Faust-book has Mephostophilis serve Faustus only with Lucifer's permission and makes him give an orthodox account of the fall, but it says nothing about 'voluntary ascent' or about the misery of the bad angels. Marlowe is responsible too for the play's distinction between Mephostophilis's negative view of evil and Faustus's belief in its positive satisfactions. We can feel the force of the distinction by emending Faustus's speech at I. iii. 101-10 and giving it to the devil—'Had you as many souls as there be stars You'd give them all for princely Lucifer', and so on. We see immediately that Mephostophilis's negative vision at this point is totally inhospitable to such innocent delusions. Faustus's confidence in the positive and substantial powers of Lucifer makes him distinctly Manichean, while Mephostophilis is Augustinian. Augustine speaks of himself 'brought down to the *depths of hell*! toiling and turmoiling', because he 'knew not that evil was nothing but a privation of good' (*Confessions*, III. 11-12).

From an Augustinian point of view, Faustus's language is still 'good' so long as it continues to express positive and exhilarating ambitions. For 'Worldly honour hath also its grace, and the power of overcoming, and of mastery' and 'The life also which here we live hath its own enchantment'. Nevertheless, Augustine might have convicted Faustus of 'an immoderate inclination towards these goods of a lower order' (*Confessions* II. 10), while philosophers would deprecate the swelling arrogance of his rhetoric, and the pious, would murmur 'the tongue is a little member and boasteth great things' (*Jas*. iii. 5).

An intimation of Faustus's fundamental situation is supplied in the scene between Wagner and the Clown (I. iv), where the Clown is offered a contract of service, and gold to appease his appetite. The travesty of the main plot is rubbed in with the joke about selling a soul to the devil for a shoulder of mutton, when the Clown (like Faustus?) would dictate terms—'I had need to have it well roasted. ... if I pay so dear'. This is what appetite and the 'conjuring occupation' boil down to at the level of street-life.

Faustus's soliloquy in the next scene marks his first commission of *despair* since he took up Jerome's Bible. Despair, the sin by which the offender disables himself from seeking grace, is a major theme of the play, through Faustus's boast of 'desperate thoughts against Jove's deity' (I. iii. 88) to Mephostophilis's ' 'tis too late, despair, farewell' (V. ii. 95). Yet it is not easy to sense, before the compact, any tense conflict of which the issue remains in doubt. Faustus tries to foreclose conflict in the opening resolution of II. i, 'Now, Faustus, must thou needs be damned'. His despair is of hope repudiated not abandoned ('Away with such vain fancies, and despair').

But Marlowe does not allow Faustus to escape altogether from a religious mode of experience. Hope and faith cannot be excluded but only diverted, as Faustus will 'Despair in God and trust in Beelzebub'. He will keep his trust in the devil unwavering ('Why waverest?') and so reverse Paul's counsel 'Let us hold fast the profession of our faith without wavering' (*Heb.* x. 23); and he uses 'go not backward' in the teeth of the Gospel's 'No man, having put his hand to the plough, and looking back, is fit for the kingdom of God' (*Luke* ix. 62). The 'something' sounding in his ears is the prompting of prevenient grace, disposing the heart to seek God, but he refuses to attend and justifies his wilfulness with false doctrine.

Augustine, under the influence of the Manichees, 'accused flesh' for his sins, maintaining that God's 'unchangeable substance did err upon constraint' rather than confess that his own 'changeable substance had gone astray voluntarily' (*Confessions*, IV. 26). Faustus is in the same state; the god he serves is his 'own appetite Wherein is fixed the love of Beelzebub'. Doubly perverse, he serves appetites that should be ruled, and uses 'fixed' to suggest that the bent of his will is pre-determined. But it is only because he is determined to be damned that he can claim his damnation determined.

The devil-may-care peremptoriness of Faustus's tone, excluding genuine perplexity whenever it is about to be admitted, adds zest to Marlowe's caricature of the moral obliquity of Faustus's thought. Some have thought the text corrupt, but a passage of sober reflection would have compelled us to take the heterodox theology more seriously, and spoiled the spectacle of scholar turned witch and grotesquely resolute to sacrifice 'the lukewarm blood of new-born babes'.

The Angels (I. iv. 14-20) again restore the audience's moral perspective. Faustus's desire for honour and wealth becomes evil as he turns his back on the Good Angel to obtain them. When the Angels retire he speaks as though he had won salvation from the devil. 'When Mephostophilis shall stand by me What power can hurt me' seems to parody 'The Lord is my light and my salvation, whom shall I fear' (*Ps.* xxvii. i), and the effect is sustained with the Biblical phrase 'glad tidings' and by the liturgical invocation to Mephostophilis. Faustus thinks that by resolution he has resolved all conflict; but after the compact his state will be more tormented than ever.

When the Angels reappear in II. ii Faustus is beginning to lose his confidence in the heroic consolations of evil and his moral distress is becoming genuine: 'My heart is hardened, I cannot repent.' The despair of 'cannot' is more poignant than the despair of 'will not', and the impression of a will paralysed by incapacity grows stronger as the play advances. The Angels precipitate the conflict now, and they set Faustus's perspective as well as the audience's. His will begins to collaborate with the promptings of the Good and struggles to defy the Bad. 'Be I a devil,' he says (with the stress on 'Be'), 'yet God may pity me'; the thought is heretical (God's mercy is not extended to devils), but its impulse is salutary and its corollary true, 'God will pity me if I repent.' Yet the Bad Angel is right too, 'Ay, but Faustus never shall repent.' We are in the territory of *The Conflict of Conscience* and the Spira story, where the hero cries, 'I am secluded clean from grace, my heart is hardened quite', and is sorely tempted to suicide, 'O, that my body were at rest, and soul in condemnation.' But Marlowe allows no appeal to the Calvinist doctrine that some are for ever 'reprobate', but chooses rather to represent the will as incapable of redeeming itself. Faustus's will assumes its power again only in 'I am resolved Faustus shall not repent'.

'Woe to the audacious soul!' says Augustine, 'which hoped, by forsaking Thee, to gain some better thing! Turned it hath, and turned again, upon back, sides and belly, yet all was painful, and Thou alone rest' (*Confessions*, VI. 25) Marlowe has Faustus turn and turn in II. ii, but does he allow him an authentic repentance? His resonant and fearful cry, 'O Christ, my saviour, my saviour! help to save distressed Faustus' soul', is mocked by the ruthless stage-direction: *Enter Lucifer, Beelzebub, and Mephostophilis.* With his characteristic love of excess, Marlowe takes a pitiless view of Faustus's plight and puts his repentance to an extreme test. Faustus fails to pass it because he cannot humiliate himself before the devil and reverts to his absurdly malignant fantasies of destruction. Vowing 'never to look at heaven', he again persuades himself that he has put an end to conflict; and, in a sense, he has.

The Testament of Faustus

After the expectation of 'glad tidings' both the matter and the manner of Mephostophilis's report (II. i. 30-36) come as tense anti-climax: the anticipated communion with the powers of evil boils down to a bargain over a legal contract of loan. Faustus has become 'a petty case of paltry legacies' (I. i. 30) conducted over the 'vain trifle' (I. iii. 61) of his soul. Earlier he tried to dictate terms as to an emissary, but now he warily seeks to make the best of a bad case as with a solicitor. As before, none of the devil's answers are reassuring. Faustus's soul will merely 'enlarge the kingdom' of Lucifer, and man is tempted only because misery loves company. The Latin hexameter expressing this last idea tolls ominously in its English setting, intimating the ultimate terms of Faustus's contract with evil and hinting at the nature of the bond between Faustus and his 'sweet Mephostophilis'. As Augustine has it, 'the devils neither conquer nor chain any man but by fellowship of sin' (*City of God*, X. xxii).

The blood-letting is a formal seal of this fellowship as well as a commitment to Lucifer (II. i. 51-55). Marlowe gives Mephistophilis a more positive part in the ritual than he has in the Faust-book, where he vanishes at the words 'o homo fuge' and leaves Faustus to warm his own blood in a saucer. Faustus in the play comes increasingly under the devil's power as he plays into his hands.

The play keeps in touch with the Biblical tradition of the solemnity of blood-covenant. Paul writes, 'where a testament is, there must also of necessity be the death of the testator', and 'almost all things are by the law purged with blood; and without shedding of blood is no remission' (*Heb.* ix). Faustus bequeaths his soul to Lucifer in the words that seal Christ's Testament on the Cross: *Consummatum est.* He perfects his travesty of Christian mystery.

Again Faustus averts conflict by 'resolution'. His blood refuses to flow, testifying to the unnaturalness of his offence. When he persists, his plea that his soul is his own is a sin against the order celebrated in *Psalm* cix, 'My soul is continually in my hand: yet do I not forget thy law'. The admonitory words *Homo fuge* (perhaps originally alluding to 1 *Tim.* vi. 11) fade and return like an hallucination of conscience; but again he meets it with brash theology ('If unto God he'll throw me down to hell') and heroic resolution ('Yet shall not Faustus fly').

The covenant signed, Mephostophilis has his first aside to the audience, 'What will not I do to obtain his soul!' It brings a new audience-relationship to bear, making the devil a cunning contriver, as so often in the old Moralities. The illusion of a candid fellowship in sin is broken, and whatever its tone (eager, ferocious or wry) it lessens the solemnity of the pact and makes it look like a diabolical joke. The blood-testament has indeed only the solemnity that Faustus endows it with; its significance (as with the conjuring) is in the blasphemy not in the efficacy of the bond, and for the Good Angel it is always without finality.

The scene recovers its routine legal formality as Faustus hands over the deed of gift in exchange for crowns and rich apparel. Greg attributes this episode (80-111) to a collaborator, and it does revert to the source. Yet there is propriety in the scene's decline into spectacular farce and in Faustus's lapse to crass indifference, 'Ay, take it, and the devil give thee good of it'.

The Immanence of Hell

Faustus's curiosity about cosmography and his contempt for conventional theology meet in his question, 'where is the place that men call hell?' The answer has always troubled theologians. In *The City of God* (XX. xvi) Augustine says, 'what or where it is I hold unknown to all but those unto whom it pleases the spirit to reveal it'; but elsewhere he says it is under the earth. The Faust-book tells of a 'confused hell' which might be expected to breed dancing devils with fireworks; in it 'is nought to find but a filthie, Sulphurish, firie, stinking mist or fog'—a tradition exploited in *Macbeth*, where 'hell is murky', and consonant enough with Augustine's view of evil as none-being.

In Mephostophilis's great speech (II. i. 117-24) Marlowe names neither the 'eternal worm' nor the 'never dying fire', but evokes the state of which they are the symbols. It is a vast and comprehensive yet intimately felt ordeal of negation, and whether it is spiritual or physical seems not to matter. The effect is won by a cogent imprecision that does not disable the expressiveness of the terse and desolating rhetoric.

'Within the bowels of these elements' seems at first to mean the bowels of the earth, or within the compass of the elemental spheres surrounding the earth. But the phrase itself refuses to be confined, and we are cheated of its simpler meanings by 'hell hath no limits'. Perhaps this means 'no precise limits', for the next lines are, as Kocher shows, consonant with Aquinas's teaching that demons suffer both in hell itself and in the 'dark atmosphere' where they tempt men (Aquinas cites a gloss on *Jas*. iii. 6, 'They carry the fire of hell with them wherever they go.') But a more mysterious idea of an uncircumscribed hell had been put foreward in Marlowe's time by the 'ubiquitist' Protestant theologian Johann Brenz, and with his doctrine in mind 'elements' may mean the stars and hell be thought to pervade the whole cosmos in a state of negative conjunction with heaven. While if 'elements' means the four material states, 'bowels' suggests a hollowness at the centre of matter.

The final lines (122-5) are about the Last Judgment and are reminiscent of 2 *Pet*. iii. 10-12, where the 'elements' and 'the earth also and the works that are therein' are 'dissolved' to make way for 'new heavens and new earth, wherein dwelleth righteousness' (see also *Mal*. iii. 2-3). Augustine speaks of 'all the world's corruptible qualities' being 'burnt away' in refining fire, and his doctrines are echoed in *The French Academy* (III. 25). Marlowe keeps his distance from the harassing material problems of Augustinian theology, but retains its key moral concept—the torment of eternal deprivation and severance from God. He expresses the ordeal of total negation without admitting the consolations of extinction and oblivion.

The *Academy* (II. 76) speaks of 'Atheists' who 'labour to persuade themselves that there is no hell nor punishment for souls after this life, but that they are only poeticall fictions and fables'. Since Mephostophilis offers no 'poetical fiction' of the conventional sort, Faustus's 'I think hell's a fable' courts the sardonic rebuke, 'Ay, think so still, till experience change thy mind.' Humanly speaking, Faustus's contentment with the routine of 'sleeping, eating, walking and disputing' (137) convicts him of gross moral torpor; he is affirming only the minimal 'goods' of life. The *Academy* would find him not precisely an Atheist but an Epicurean.

The Power and the Glory

After the compact the devil can keep his part of the bargain. He can offer Faustus, who has bowed down and worshipped him, the 'kingdoms of the world and the glory of them'. Marlowe does not allow us to forget the Gospel question, 'what shall it profit a man if he shall gain the whole world, and lose his own soul?', but nor do we forget, in the words of the Sanctus, that 'The heavens and all the earth are full of the majesty of Thy glory'. The perspectives of the play are changed and so are the terms of its conflict, but it keeps a certain continuity.

Lust and Desire

Mixing the service of God with the service of Mammon, like the hero of the Faust-book, Faustus 'wanton and lascivious' asks for a wife. Mephostophilis, reversing normal values, supplies him with a devil-wife whom Faustus rejects as a 'hot whore'. The popular joke at the expense of the sanctity of marriage is quite transcended, however, as the devil, beginning with a superbly condescending aphorism—'Marriage is but a ceremonial toy'—enlarges on the virtues of his 'fairest courtesans' (II. i. 149-56). They are endowed with all the fabulous sanctities—the chastity of Penelope, the wisdom of Saba (Queen of Sheba) and the beauty of Lucifer 'before his fall'. In heaven, we may remember, there will be no marriage or giving in marriage, the redeemed are 'as the angels of God in heaven' (*Mat.* xxii. 30). These courtesans are sacred virgins, and it is a tribute to the verse that the phrase 'every morning' does not make us think of the self-indulgence of a lecherous stayabed, but of the aptness of the morning's purity and promise and of the unfallen Lucifer as 'son of the morning'.

Mephostophilis now is using rhetoric to sustain Faustus's heroic illusions about evil; through emancipation from law man may recover the delights of paradise before the fall. His sudden transition from women to gold ('The iterating of these lines brings gold') is not a sign of a defect in the text, but a stepping from one sanctity to another, as it were from the Song of Solomon to Solomon's wealth and power (see 2 *Chron.* ix).

These divine prospects are kept open when we are told of blind Homer singing 'Of Alexander's love and Oenon's death', and of Amphion, who 'With ravishing sound of his melodious harp' makes music with Mephostophilis (II. ii. 24-29). The 'sweet pleasure' that conquers 'deep despair' is evidently the poetic *furore*. But, while Mephostophilis

commands the music, the prospects it opens seem not to be in his do-
main; they are tantalising glimpses of unrealised possibilities of life and
of the bliss that the damned have lost for ever. The more ecstatic
rhetoric of the play is poignantly nostalgic—a reaching upwards to a
transfigured sensuality. Simon, one feels, would have understood both
the vision of the courtesans and the address to Helen.

When Lucifer comes in person to entertain Faustus he offers him the spectacle not of transfigured but of disfigured sensuality. He presents a Moral-
ity-pageant of the Seven Deadly Sins which Marlowe uses to express his
own Augustinian view of evil as the negation of life and all its dynamic
desires. The wench that Pride enjoys has nothing high about her but her
smell; Covetousness spawns gold in an old churl's leather bag; the bastard
Envy wishes all books burned; Wrath wounds itself for want of an enemy;
Gluttony menaces Faustus's victuals; Sloth, exhausted by other vices, is
rendered incapable of speech; and Lechery's love of life is reduced to a
preference for raw meat over dried fish, with a repulsive bawdy quibble.

The Deadly Sins in medieval plays (e.g. *Mary Magdalene*) usually put
up a better case for themselves, and Faustus's cry 'Oh, how this sight doth
delight my soul' might have seemed inexplicable as well as ironic, were
it not that his exultant disgust springs from his enjoyment of sharing the
privilege of Lucifer's throne (like a royal guest) and being superior to the
vices that overtake mankind. He asks to visit hell and return safely, but
hell has already visited him and left him contaminated.

The Secrets of Astronomy

When Faustus, showing a legitimate interest in the created world,
reasons with Mephostophilis about 'divine astrology' Marlowe takes the
opportunity to educate his audience, as the author of *The Four Elements*
had done before him. It used to be thought that Marlowe not only ignored the helio-centric Copernican system (which was little known at
the time) but also the widely accepted current modifications of the
Ptolemaic geo-centric account. But F. R. Johnson has more recently
claimed that he presents 'an unorthodox sixteenth-century modification
of the current astronomy'.[1]

[1] Francis Johnson, 'Marlowe's Astronomy and Renaissance Scepticism',
English Literary History 13, 1946. For the view that Mephistophilis's
astronomy is unorthodox see Howard Schultz, *Milton and Forbidden
Knowledge* (1955).

Marlowe's knowledge of astronomical theories, however, might have been wholly derived from *The French Academy*, whose third volume (published in English after Marlowe's death, but available in French) deals with Good and Evil Angels, the Celestial Spheres, elemental meterology, and the flora and fauna of the earth. Its astronomy is reasonably lucid and does much to illuminate the play. Faustus starts by asking, 'Are all celestial bodies but one globe, As is the substance of this centric earth?' (II. ii. 34). The *Academy* would answer, 'The stars are nothing else but certain firm, clear and solid parts of their heavens, made in round form.' Mephostophilis's reply is much too comprehensive for the question and summarises much else in the *Academy* account. The 'elements' with which he compares the 'heavens' are the elemental spheres at the centre of the cosmos (i.e. the earth, surrounded by water, air and fire); they are 'mutually enfolded' because all the spheres are concentric; and they move 'upon one axle tree' because all the heavenly spheres share the same diurnal motion. The allusion to the 'names' of Saturn, Mars and Jupiter, a bit obscure in the play, is explained in the *Academy*: 'And for Saturn, Jupiter, Mars ... they are especially named planets, that is wandering in their motions', and, to help the ignorant, Astrologers 'have also named and represented these stars by personages of divers habits and countenances'. Each of the planetary spheres and the lunar sphere has in addition to its diurnal motion, its 'own natural and peculiar motion contrary to the first and on other poles and axes'. The play accords, and Faustus gives the accepted times for the planetary and lunar orbits except for Mars, which is inexplicably given as four years instead of two.

Passing from 'freshmen's suppositions' to more critical matters, Faustus learns that each sphere has its own 'dominion' or *intelligentia*; that there are nine spheres, including the motionless 'empyreal heaven' and that the *coelum igneum* and *crystallinum* are 'fables'. The *Academy* discusses the possibility of each sphere having an 'intelligence', but finds the truth of the matter hidden from man; it gives the same 'commonly received' account of eight moving spheres; it discusses the 'Empyreal Heaven', which is 'vital, flaming and divine' and receives 'the souls of the blessed'; it wonders about the existence of a crystal sphere; and it gives a chapter to the view that 'there is no fire under the orb of the moon' (i.e. no *coelum igneum*). It also attributes the irregular frequency of conjunctions and eclipses to the 'variety of motions' of heavenly bodies; but Mephostophilis's Latin (meaning 'by their unequal motion in respect to the whole') has not been traced to a specific source.

It is likely, therefore, that Marlowe's astronomy was commonplace to the well-informed; the *Academy* would allow the devil's answers as probable enough, and indeed pious in accepting the 'empyreal heaven', which was more the concern of theologians than astronomers. But it is possible, as Johnson argues, that Marlowe knew that by allowing only eight moving spheres and attributing an 'intelligence' to each, he was approving the 'advanced' theories of Ricius. Ricius rejected the crystal sphere because he saw that the 'trepidation' it was supposed to account for was an illusory phenomenon owed to faulty successive measurements of the precession of the equinoxes. He also rejected the *primum mobile* or 'first mover', which Aristotle had identified with the firmament and Ptolemy had separated off to account for precession; he preferred the theory of 'intelligences' not because it was held by many theologians but because it seemed to him the simplest and most rational explanation of the several kinds of heavenly motion.

The less-technical astronomy in the chorus opening Act III mentions the *primum mobile* without hinting at its nature, and it might raise doubts about the coherence and seriousness of Marlowe's knowledge. There is, however, no doubt about the dramatic significance of the astronomy, both when it seems technical and when it seems rhetorical. Faustus is out to 'find the secrets of astronomy Graven in the book of Jove's high firmament'. He mounts 'to scale Olympus' top', and heaven will conspire his overthrow.

The Kingdoms of the World

When, at the start of Act III, Faustus goes 'to prove cosmography That measures coasts and kingdoms of the earth', the *Academy* would approve his passage from astronomy to geography while lamenting his dangerous 'curiosity in knowledge' and even his 'curiosity of seeing strange nations' (Bk. I. 15). It seems that the Faust-book translator was also guilty of this last offence, for the opening speeches of III. i closely follow a passage he added to the German original; he indulges his own delight in Europe's wonders, and Marlowe had only to recast the prose into verse. Where, for example, the source has 'there saw he the Tombe of Virgil; & the high way that he cutte through that mighty hill of stone in one night, the whole length of an English mile', the play reads, 'There saw we learned

Maro's golden tomb, The way he cut, an English mile in length, Thorough a rock of stone in one night's space'. The middle of the play is often an efficient re-hashing of the source, but, as in these opening speeches, Marlowe often insinuates something of his own. Faustus's last appeal to Mephostophilis before the Pope enters (III. i. 70-77), for example, touches the source material with a Simonian and Renaissance delight in flight and remoteness ('So high our dragons soared into the air' and so on), remembers the temptation of Christ ('There did we view the kingdoms of the world') and triumphantly returns to the prospect of the play: 'Then in this show let me an actor be, That this proud Pope may Faustus' cunning see.' The tone promises (or threatens) something resembling the boisterous and alarming caricature of *The Jew of Malta*, and the audience is not disappointed.

The Papal Dignity

Simon could challenge Peter before Nero in Rome, but Faustus, to accomplish the same design, had to cross Europe. The play supplies an ingenious link between Papal and Imperial scenes by culling from Foxe's *Book of Martyrs* (or from an unknown source) a few excuses for presenting a quarrel between the Pope at Rome and the Emperor with his nominee Bruno. The play's Pope 'Adrian' may owe his name to Hadrian VI, a contemporary of the historical Faustus, or to Hadrian IV, who also quarrelled with the Emperor; but he owes his arrogance to his progenitor in the play, Alexander III, who succeeded Hadrian IV. The historical Frederick Barbarossa set up a rival Pope (Victor IV), but Alexander eventually triumphed and, it is said, literally set his foot upon the Emperor's neck and quoted *Psalm* xci (compare III. i. 136-42). The play's choice of the name 'Bruno' is probably arbitrary; the earlier Brunos who became Popes (as Gregory V and Leo IX) are remote in time and circumstance, and nothing is gained by assuming a sly allusion to Giordano Bruno.

Marlowe took the opportunity to caricature the hubristic violence of the history of the Papacy and the Empire, and while much is in the manner of Protestant Interlude and its later developments (e.g. *The Troublesome Reign of King John*), there is some of the grotesque rhetoric and gull-and-knave comedy that Ben Jonson was to develop (for instance Mephostophilis's speech immediately before the Pope's entrance).

The knavery of Faustus and Mephostophilis is a moral purgative; the

D

devil and his angel overreach the pride of the Pope as it is vaunted over the 'haughty insolence' of the Emperor. This is one way of coming to terms with evil; in a world in which authority is flouted, the lesser knave is gulled by the greater and a kind of justice done for ironists to enjoy. Just as the tragedy is precisely focused on the presumption of man, so too is the comedy. Tragedy, remembering that man is mortal, makes death confound his pride of life; comedy, remembering that human life goes on, humiliates the man who affects to be superior to his fellows. The Pope's words will serve as motto to both sides of the play:

> He grows too proud in his authority,
> Lifting his lofty head above the clouds,
> And like a steeple overpeers the church;
> But we'll pull down his haughty insolence.

Marlowe clowns to a purpose.

The World's Regard

Faustus's performances before the Emperor are without the bizarre and outrageous quality of the anti-papist antics. Sticking to its source, the play lapses into its uncritical allegiances to civil authority. The addition of the Bruno episode makes things worse, since we are not expected to see any irony in the patriotic piety of 'poor Faustus' when he promises to 'Both love and serve the German Emperor And lay his life at holy Bruno's feet'. After the imperial ambitions voiced early in the play, Faustus's exercise of the privileges of power is disappointing. It is, of course, appropriate that it should be; but Marlowe does not sufficiently bring home to us the nature of the disappointment and betrayal. The scenes remind us that great magicians (even Simon and Cornelius Agrippa) are at best reputable court entertainers and not masters of empire. But Marlowe was evidently not much interested in the arts they practised or the whims they satisfied, and only at one point does he turn his scepticism and indifference into calculated dramatic bathos—where the Emperor, to 'satisfy' his 'longing thoughts at full' asks to see the 'little wart or mole'on the neck of Alexander's paramour. 'Patient judgments' may here recognise a trivial appetite for 'curiosity and novelty'; but for the greater part of the act this is the only taste that the play itself tries to satisfy.

The sport at the expense of Benvolio (mainly from the Faust-book) keeps alive something of the play's concern with heroic vanity (particularly at the start of IV. iii), but the plenitude of horns hardly compensates for the emptiness of Marlowe's horn of plenitude. The low-life scenes (III. iii; IV. v, vi, vii) are likewise, as Faustus puts it, when he brings them to a crisis in the Emperor's court, 'good subject for a merriment'. Robin, Dick, the Carter, the horse-courser and the Hostess are simple people at the mercy of the *magus*; their punishments, aptly administered to 'saucy varlets' who try to get the better of supernatural power, make 'artful sport' to drive away the 'sad thoughts' of the courtiers. They try, as Mephostophilis says of Faustus, 'To overreach the devil, but all in vain'.

'Vain' is perhaps the key-word for the impression given by the fourth act. It expresses what Faustus will call 'the vain pleasure of four and twenty years'. But in the course of the act the vanity, with shoulder-shrugging good humour, is as often indulged as exposed. Were it otherwise, the last act would perhaps be less impressive in calling Faustus and the audience to final account.

The Damnation of Faustus

Pico, in his *Oration*, recalls 'that it was a saying of Zoroaster that the soul is winged and that, when the wings drop off, she falls again into the body; and then, after her wings have grown again sufficiently, she flies back to heaven'. After his headlong fall into the body, Faustus's wings seem to grow again in the last act.

The Vision of Helen

When 'music sounds' and Helen passes across the stage her sanctity is mirrored in the awed calm of the scholars' judgments. Her 'heavenly beauty passeth all compare'; she is 'the pride of nature's work' and a 'blessed sight'. This vision lends intensity and compassion to the austere admonitions of the Old Man, who speaks to Faustus when the scholars have left. Marlowe anticipates Milton in finding a poetry of 'kind rebuke', a moral music, to efface the magic that charms the soul to hell. And in the Scholar's 'Too simple is my wit to tell her praise' and the Old Man's 'No mortal can express the pains of hell', he seems to set himself new tasks for language to perform.

When Faustus resumes his communion with Helen the context in the scene and the play calls for an extreme and simultaneous celebration of the rival values of the heroic and moral orders; and this is accomplished with marvellous economy. From a moral point of view Faustus's will is viciously egocentric: 'let me crave of thee To glut the longing of my heart's desire'; and his eagerness to 'extinguish clear Those thoughts that do dissuade me from my vow' is a manifest sin against the Holy Spirit. And yet it is a dedicated will, and the self seems transcended by the sanctity of its aspiration and allegiance. Thoughts that would dissuade from a vow to a seemingly unfallen Lucifer are extinguished for the sake of clearness and purity, and the 'sweet embracings' of 'heavenly Helen' suggest a divine wedding in the mode of the *Song of Solomon* rather than (for example) the whoredoms of Samaria and Jerusalem in *Ezekiel* (xxiii).

Mephostophilis performs his last trick 'in twinkling of an eye'. Is Marlowe recalling St. Paul? 'In a moment, in the twinkling of an eye, at the last trump: for the trumpet shall sound, and the dead shall be raised incorruptible ... this mortal must put on immortality' (I *Cor.* xv. 52).

When Helen comes again in pageant style 'between two Cupids' Marlowe endows Faustus with Tamburlaine's and Dido's passions for heroic immortality. Tamburlaine had remembered from 'Homer's Iliads', '*Hellen*, whose beauty sommond Greece to armes, And drew a thousand ships to *Tenedos*' (2 *Tamb.* 3054). Dido recalls 'the thousand ships' that desolated Troy and cries that her lover will make her 'immortall with a kisse', while Aeneas calls waves 'topless hills' and speaks of a thousand Grecians 'in whose sterne faces shin'd the quenchless fire, That after burnt the pride of *Asia*' (*Dido*, 1612, 1329, 1162, 481). Marlowe tells Helen's praises by recalling from the heroic past the power that moved on her behalf and, endowing the scholar with a soldier's imagination, he allows Faustus's resolution to renew it for the future: 'And I will combat with weak Menelaus And wear thy colours on my plumed crest.' We feel too that Marlowe is vindicating his time's innocent love of tournament and chivalry.

But rival feelings are awakened also. Without alluding to the Old Testament, Marlowe moves in the same territories of the imagination, and feels Ezekiel's fascination for conjunctions of beauty, passion and destruction (see *Ez.* xxiii). Unlike the Sabean harlots, Helen is divine; but the sacking of Troy and Wittenberg for her sake is related to the Biblical image of the refining fire purging precious metals: 'All is dross that is not Helena.' The speech looks back not only to Valdes on 'the queen of love', Faustus's hope to 'live in all voluptuousness' and the Prologue's exequy to 'proud audacious deeds' but also to Mephostophilis's Last Judgment 'when all the world dissolves And every creature shall be purified'. The purity is characteristically evoked by 'the evening's air', 'a thousand stars', 'flaming Jupiter' and 'wanton Arethusa's azured arms', reconciling 'sweet pleasure' with Faustus's delight in beholding the heavens.

When Faustus kisses Helen he reconciles present with future satisfactions—the large Romantic cry 'I will'. Shakespeare's Cleopatra will say 'Eternity was in our lips and eyes', and Blake that 'The Gates of the Senses open upon Eternity'; and Marlowe here persuades us that Gluttony and Lechery have carried Faustus through hell to a prospect of Heaven. 'Her lips suck forth my soul' may make Faustus a witch and Helen a succuba, but 'see where it flies!' is a Simonian cry of triumph. Marlowe will not easily over-reach his own verbal magic.

The Plight of the Man

Faustus is 'but a man condemned to die' (IV. v. 21), 'has offended like a man' (V. i. 40) and has a 'distressed soul' (V. i. 65). His plight is expressed in a scrap of soliloquy, in his dealings with the Old Man and in his last talk with the scholars.

The comedy requires that Faustus should fall asleep and lose his leg (IV. v), and the opportunity is taken to remind us that his 'fatal' time draws to a final end. His distress is intense, but its nature uncertain—we cannot tell if the 'distrust' that despair drives into his thoughts is of God or of the devil. The passions of conscience, however, are in any case salutary, and Faustus is to blame for (very humanly) trying to 'confound' them with a quiet sleep. Sleep, like sloth, can be a sin. Faustus settles down for a nap in the hope of dodging moral conflict; and his 'Tush, Christ did call the thief upon the cross' is not as Greg supposes 'a sentimental piety' but a complacent blasphemy; in the Spira story and play the same sentiment is gravely weighed.

The Old Man's compassionate censure of Faustus adds a new dimension to our sense of the human predicament: 'Yet, yet, thou hast an amiable soul If sin by custom grow not into nature.' Augustine says, 'For the law of sin is the violence of custom, whereby the mind is drawn and holden, even against its will; but deservedly, for that it willingly fell into it

(*Confessions* VIII. 12). Faustus is in this state of being 'deservedly' held against will. Yet it is a bitter irony that the will in its freedom can more readily fall than climb. In putting so strong a stress on the will, it is easy to court the Pelagian heresy, which held that the human will can win salvation without grace. Marlowe encounters some difficulty in distinguishing dramatically between repentance by an act of free will and repentance through grace. The Old Man dissuades Faustus from using the devil's dagger by telling him of a hovering angel 'with a vial full of precious grace' and pleading with him to 'call for mercy and avoid despair'. Is it that Faustus cannot repent because he is without grace, and cannot have grace because he will not repent? Or is it that he cannot receive the grace of justification from the angelic vial because he has too often denied the promptings of prevenient grace? Either way, the human relationship has its own dignity and power, and leaves us to wonder why a graceless man should be so moved by another's compassion.

As 'hell strives with grace' for conquest in Faustus's breast, the powers of light and darkness seem matched in the Manichean way. But to patient judgment it appears that Faustus's yielding to evil is voluntary, while the Old Man's resistance to it makes it assist in the perfection of virtue. Faustus is again trapped by the metaphor of Lucifer as 'sovereign lord' with Mephostophilis an emissary empowered to punish a 'traitor'. He can only conceive 'presumption' as an offence against the tyranny of Pride, and it is his own pride that commits him to 'proud Lucifer'. The same pride moves his address to Helen with its presumptions of immortality and magnificence; it would be admirable were it not a last vain bid to escape from the human condition as the Old Man represents it. In the futility of his pride Faustus commands that the 'base and aged man' should suffer the 'greatest torments that our hell Affords'.

But the Old Man triumphantly endures the torments that in this life pride inflicts on humility. 'Satan begins to sift me with his pride' recalls *Luke* xxii. 31, 'Satan hath desired to have you, that he may sift you as wheat'. It is another image of purifying ordeal, and it is suffered on earth in 'our hell'—'As in this furnace God shall try my faith' (see *Is.* xlviii. 10). The Old Man will 'fly unto God' while the scholar Faustus remains below. As Augustine has it, 'The unlearned start up and take heaven by force, and we with our learning, and without heart, lo, where we wallow in flesh and blood.' (*Confessions*, VIII. 19).

When Lucifer and his henchmen take up their positions to witness

Faustus's end they are like the figures of revenge-play (e.g. *The Spanish Tragedy*) who gloat upon the ironic justice they exact from men. Here, however, as Mephostophilis looks forward to a spectacle of 'desperate lunacy' as man's 'labouring brain' begets 'idle fantasies To overreach the devil', the gloating takes the form of a pitiless objectivity about the nature of evil.

But the talk with the scholars supplies no 'idle fantasies' as Faustus movingly reassumes his humanity and his fellowship with other men. Yet both are flawed by his isolation and sense of his unique doom: 'had I lived with thee, then had I lived still'. We recognise humility stirring in his courtesy, but his resolute apartness is subtly touched with pride. He blames the devils for the paralysis of his moral being: 'I would weep, but the devil draws in my tears. ... I would lift up my hands, but see, they hold 'em, they hold 'em'; but when the scholars chorus 'Who Faustus?' we are more persuaded of the reality of the incapacities for grief and penitence than of the power of the invisible spirits. Self-assertion and self-effacement meet in, 'Talk not of me, but save yourselves and depart'; as in the will he leaves for Wagner, there is a touch of irony in his magnanimity. And there is keen pathos in his farewell as it salvages a last pretext of reassurance, 'If I live till morning I'll visit you.'

A Last Judgment

After the scholars have left, the mockery of Mephostophilis administers a last turn of the screw: ' 'Twas I, that when thou wert i' the way to heaven, Dammed up thy passage; when thou tookst the book To view the scriptures, then I turned the leaves And led thine eye.' Faustus weeps. It is a terrifying speech, recoiling upon our whole experience of the play. But without it the exploration of the mystery of evil would not be complete; it is the dramatic equivalent of the Gospel's equally disturbing, 'Then entered Satan into Judas' (*Luke* xxii. 3). From one point of view the play's devils are only symbols of 'aspiring pride and insolence', and it is simply Faustus's wilful pride that turned the leaves and led his eye. It is *as if* the devil were directing him. But when Christianity externalised and personalised pride in its dramatic mythology of Satan it exposed itself to the hazard it meets here: man is prey to an adversary whose power daunts even Faustus and, as we have seen, daunted even Peter in his contests with Simon. In the tragic tradition, Satan's power is like a malignant fate (man is punished for the pride he was born with); in the

Morality tradition it has grown into an inexplicable challenge to the power and mercy of God.

Yet the Good Angel denies the devil's ultimate power over man: 'Hadst thou affected sweet dinity Hell or the devil had had no power on thee'; and Faustus's failure to affect divinity is manifestly voluntary and culpable. But whether we take Mephostophilis's claim literally or metaphorically, we are left to repeat Augustine's unanswerable question: 'what can cause the will's evil, the will being sole cause of all evil?'

The final angelic pronouncements are, as Greg says, a Last Judgment upon Faustus. After it Faustus's death is not the natural death of the body only, but also what Augustine calls 'the eternal, penal second death' (referred to in *Rev.* xx. 14), and his soul tumbles directly into 'confusion'. The hell-fire and the tormented glutton of the Bad Angel's description retain their traditional power (see *Luke* xvi. 24) and there is no need to attribute them to a collaborator.

Damned Perpetually

Faustus's great final soliloquy consummates the play in both its aspects —Morality and Heroic Tragedy—and each in its own way triumphs over the other. In fear we acquiesce in the littleness and powerlessness of man, and in pity we share his sufferings and endorse his protest.

The horrible prospect of a man being burnt alive, which Marlowe (like the Christianity he honours) does not spare us, accounts for little of the pathos and power. In the first lines we are much more moved by the magnificent futility of the human protest against the inexorable movement of time as it enacts an inexorable moral law. We are reminded that 'all things that move between the quiet poles' are at the command of the process Faustus would escape: the 'ever-moving spheres' cannot by definition 'stand still'. Faustus had explained the seasonal 'circles' to the Duchess, who marvelled at the winter grapes (IV. vii. 23), and he had numbered the cycles of the spheres, but now his knowledge is of a different order. The cosmic rhythms evoked by the sense of the poetry seem to hold dominion over its movement. The first equably stressed eleven words echo the striking clock—'Ah Faustus, Now hast thou but one bare hour to live'; the 'perpetually' that falls with finality at the end of the first sentence returns in the mocking oxymoron 'perpetual day'; and 'rise, rise again' invokes precisely the diurnal motion it seeks to arrest.

The irony of the quotation from Ovid has long been celebrated. In the *Amores* (I. xiii. 40) it is the plea of ecstatic love, *Clamares*, '*lente currite, noctis equi*', which Marlowe had poorly translated, 'Then wouldst thou cry, stay night and runne not thus.' But here the Latin words in their English setting sound like a last attempt to cast a spell whose vanity is betrayed by the rhythm as the horses seem to quicken pace through the line, and confessed in 'the stars move still, time' runs, the clock will strike'. Were the soliloquy to end here we should feel that confinement to time is the cruellest fact of man's condition.

In the next lines, however, his ordeal is confinement to earth: 'Oh, I'll leap up to my God! Who pulls me down?' The image affirming the immensity of Christ's Testament also declares its unreachable remoteness: 'See see where Christ's blood streams in the firmament.' Marlowe may be remembering both the gulf between heaven and hell (*Luke* xvi. 26) and Tamburlaine, defiant in his mortal sickness:

> Come let us march against the powers of heaven,
> And set blacke streamers in the firmament,
> To signify the slaughter of the Gods.
> Ah friends, what shall I do? I cannot stand. (2 *Tamb.* 4441)

Christ has accomplished the triumph over mortality that Tamburlaine's labouring brain could only imagine. The imperial pageant hyperbole of the earlier play has in the later been made to express the superhuman power of Christ; but he conquers by sacrifice not by slaughter—humility has become heroic. Even without appeal to Christian symbolism, the play has made the streaming blood emblematic of eternal life. Blood refuses to flow when Faustus cuts his arm, it 'dries with grief' as his 'conscience kills it', and it gushes forth from his eyes 'instead of tears'. As Faustus pleads that 'one drop' then 'half a drop' would save his soul, he confesses his barren littleness of life in the vastness of the moral universe.

As the vision of blood fades, Faustus meets the unappeased wrath of God and cries for the mountains and hills to fall on him (see, e.g., *Luke* xxiii. 30, *Rev.* vi. 16, *Hos.* x. 8). Burial in earth becomes a privilege refused to the last paroxysms of Faustus's will. He is again re-enacting the fall of Lucifer, the figure in Isaiah who is 'brought down to hell, to the sides of the pit' and 'cast out of the grave like an abominable branch'

(*Is.* xiv). When Faustus hopes for a refining ordeal of dissolution and rebirth in 'the entrails of yon labouring clouds' which might 'vomit forth' his limbs and let his soul 'ascend to heaven' his words seem haunted by Lucifer's—'I will ascend above the heights of the clouds, I will be like the Most High'; and the same chapter could supply the stretching arm of God and the smoke of the Last Day (*Is.* xiv). Marlowe has assimilated and re-created the Biblical imagery, however, and it is dramatically valid whether or not we suppose it allusive. Faustus, the damned hero as the play has fashioned him, has become the fittest witness of apocalyptic vision. No chorus could speak with such moving authority, for Faustus alone has enacted all the futilities of pride.

The first phase of the soliloquy discovers the futility of human pretensions to power in the face of overwhelming cataclysm, the second makes us feel the futility of knowledge and speculation. Faustus's plea for 'some end to my incessant pain' (recalling the Faust-book and the Spira story and play) sums up that side of the Christian tradition which, with Augustine, is 'Against those that exclude both men and devils from pain eternal' (*City of God*, XXII. xxiii). Like 'Pythagoras' metempsychosis' it is wishful thinking. *The French Academy* (II. 85) could have occasioned the allusion to Pythagoras and supplied the distinction between the souls of brutes (made of 'elements') and those of men ('created of nothing'). And it would challenge Faustus's readiness to accuse the stars that reigned at his nativity by asking, 'how should the heavens, stars and planets give that to the soul which they themselves have not?' (II. 87).

Faustus moderates his struggle to escape the pain of responsibility as he curses his parents (see *Luke* xxiii. 29) and then checks himself: 'No Faustus, curse thyself, curse Lucifer That hath deprived thee of the joys of heaven.' Again, if we read 'Lucifer' as a metaphor for Pride, the problem of responsibility recedes; but it returns when we think of the devil as a person and evil as a power outside the consciousness of man. In either case, it is fitting that the pride of knowledge should be finally purged with 'I'll burn my books!' and the fellowship of sin perpetuated with 'Ah Mephostophilis!'

In the last scene, as in Shakespeare's tragedies, normal life must resume as best it can. Marlowe (there is no need to suppose a collaborator) abstains from the grotesque nastiness of the Faust-book catastrophe, and strikes an apt balance between horror, dismay and due reverence. If the noise that the scholars report seems a concession to popular taste, we may reflect that it might be a clue to the acting of Faustus's closing words, from 'My God, my God! Look not so fierce on me', and remember *Psalm* xxii:

> My God, my God, why hast thou forsaken me? why art thou so far from helping me, and from the words of my roaring?

GREAT WITS are sure to madness near allied - - - -

Epilogue

The Epilogue seals both the Heroic-play and the Morality. In 'Cut is the bough that might have grown full straight' we feel that the pruning has been done to maiming purpose. Marlowe may have remembered the image from Churchyard's *Shore's Wife*, where it also suggests wanton destruction, 'And bent the wand that mought have grown full streight'. But the Bible haunts the lines too, and the branch may be dead because it has failed to take nourishment from the tree (see *John* xv. 4-7, *Psalm* lxxx). The next line, 'And burned is Apollo's laurel bough' alludes perhaps to the frustration of Faustus's pre-eminence in the hidden mysteries, but again the destruction may be wanton. The last lines are a due and weighty warning against emulating 'forward wits' who 'practise more than heavenly power permits'; yet they leave the wise still to wonder at the enticing deepness of unlawful things.

Faustus's ordeal is specifically that of the aspiring mind (the 'unsatiable speculator' as the Faust-book has it), of that part of our nature which is dissatisfied with being merely human and tries vainly to come to rest in fantasies of omnipotence and omniscience. It is a romantic agony which oscillates across an abyss between extremities of hope and despair. Marlowe, seeing it for what it was, related the hope to the imperial and speculative ambitions of his time, and the despair to that side of Christianity which brings home to us the inescapable mortality and doom of man. Goethe, in a self-confessedly romantic age, was independently to take up the story again and, after mány oscillations, endorse its potential of hope. Marlowe stuck to the basic shape of the story and accepted the damnation of his hero. But not complacently. D. H. Lawrence, who also understood the value of extreme commitments, said that a work of art 'must contain the essential criticism on the morality to which it adheres. And hence the antinomy, hence the conflict necessary to every tragic conception.' *Dr. Faustus* adheres to the rich and searching morality of Augustinian thought; but it does not allow us to come comfortably to rest in it. In the Heroic-play the reaching mind that is punished by hell is also the mind that apprehends heaven, and Faustus—the playwright's figment—suffers the one and glimpses the other on the audience's behalf.

APPENDIX

Text, Date and Authorship

The earliest extant version of *Dr. Faustus*, known as the A-text, was published in 1604 and reprinted in 1609 and 1611; the later B-text went through six editions between 1616 and 1631. The text used for the present essay is the conjectural reconstruction put together from both texts by W. W. Greg. The A-text, he argues, was probably prepared by actors for a provincial performance during the plague-years 1592-94; lacking the prompt-book, they worked from memory until they had a version fit for a small company and a 'vulgar audience'. The B-text he believes a collation of the A-text with incomplete and hardly legible 'foul papers'. The A-text, however, is sometimes better because it includes revision made to improve the acting version, and because the B-text copy was confused by first-draft revisions and by an editor who cut profanities and tried some tidying-up of his own. Although it is hard to see why the supposedly garbled report of the A-text should preserve so much of what we value in the play, the general theory works well when brought to bear on the detail.

Most editors used to favour an early date for the play—between *Tamburlaine* (1587) and *The Jew of Malta* (1590), but Greg argues for 1592. The allusion to the Prince of Parma (I. i. 91) dates the action to 1579-90, and the Antwerp bridge was burnt by fire-ships in 1585 (I. i. 94); but neither allusion would be beyond recollection in 1592. Some lines are caught up from the play in the anonymous *Taming of a Shrew* (*c.* 1589); but this is so spurious and messy a text that arguments derived from it carry no conviction. An allusion in the *Black Book* (1604) hints at a Shoreditch Theatre performance of *Dr. Faustus* in 1590-91; but it allows us to assume that the performance took place during an intermission of the plague (1592-94). Greene's *Friar Bacon and Friar Bungay* (*c.* 1589) has been supposed an imitation of Marlowe, but the debt may have been the other way. Marlowe's immediate source, the English Faust-book, seems to have been first published in 1592, and after unsuccessful attempts to prove it in existence earlier, those who favour an early date for the play have had to make the unverifiable assumption that the manuscript was circulated in private.

The first editions of both texts ascribe the play to Marlowe alone, but the 1619 title-page adds the words 'With new Additions'. It used to be thought that the additions distinguishing the B-text from the A were those that the manager Henslowe paid Samuel Rowley and William Birde to supply to 'doctor fostes' in 1602; but Greg has shown that traces of the 'new' passages survive in the A-test, and they are therefore not additions but restorations. We are thus left without external evidence to identify any hand other than Marlowe's. Using the uncertain internal evidence, Greg suggests that Rowley may have been the original collaborator. But in the circumstances it is better to let the authorship question rest. We ought to hesitate to say with Shaw's Fanny, 'You don't expect me to know what to say about a play when I don't know who the author is, do you?'

There is no need to think of the 'lost' original as a finely organised whole of which we now catch only occasional glimpses. It is in keeping with what we know of Marlowe's plays after *Tamburlaine* to suppose that improvisation and speed left their mark from the beginning, and since the first recorded performance was in September 1594, eighteen months after Marlowe's death, it may be that he never brought his work to the stage. The date of the play may be thought to affect our view of Marlowe's development. But we may accept *Dr. Faustus* as his last play while still seeing it as a sequel to and consummation of *Tamburlaine*. Marlowe may have seen in the Faust-book an opportunity to return with greater insight to the issues that first engaged his interest in the theatre. Strictly speaking, 'did Marlowe write this?' is a question of copyright; but it is hard in practice to distinguish it from the literary question, 'does this contribute to the distinction of the play?' To answer the second question, however, may not be to meet the first; for a collaborator may have accomplished something in Marlowe's manner and Marlowe himself have made use of the clichés of the form in which he was working. And if a collaborator was responsible for the more routine passages it does not follow that Marlowe scorned them; the conjunction of Marlowe's vision with the conventions of popular moral entertainment is as the finished sculpture with the rough rock.

Further Reading

Of critical commentary on *Dr. Faustus*, most use has been made of:—

P. H. Kocher, *Christopher Marlowe* (1946)
H. Levin, *The Overreacher* (1954)

Other valuable contributions to the discussion of the play include:—

Una Ellis-Fermor, *Christopher Marlowe* (1927), and *The Frontiers of Drama* (1945)
M. C. Bradbrook, *Themes and Conventions of Elizabethan Tragedy* (1935)
N. D'Agostino, *Marlowe* (1950)
M. Poirier, *Marlowe* (1951)
P. Henderson, *Marlowe* (1952)
F. P. Wilson, *Marlowe and the Early Shakespeare* (1952)
J. C. Smith, 'Marlowe's *Dr. Faustus*', *Scrutiny VIII* 1939
L. Kirschbaum, 'Marlowe's *Faustus*', *Review of English Studies* XIX 1943
W. W. Greg, 'The Damnation of Faustus', *Modern Language Review* XLI 1946
J. C. Maxwell, 'The Sin of Faustus', *The Wind and the Rain* IV 1947